# THE ULTIMATE PRIORITY

# THE ULTIMATE PRIORITY

## JOHN MACARTHUR, JR.

# ON WORSHIP

**MOODY PRESS**

CHICAGO

All Scripture quotations in this book, except those noted otherwise, are from the *New American Standard Bible*, © 1960, 1962, 1963, 1968, 1971, 1972, 1973, 1975, and 1977 by The Lockman Foundation, and are used by permission.

**Library of Congress Cataloging in Publication Data**

MacArthur, John F.
    The ultimate priority.

    1. Worship.    I. Title.
BV10.2.M23 1983        248.3        83-5420
ISBN: 0-8024-0186-4

19 20 18

*Printed in the United States of America*

# Contents

To Dale and Lorraine Smith
on their Fiftieth Anniversary,
with gratitude that they
have given the Savior their
lives and me their daughter

# Preface

The psalmist affirms the ultimate priority for man by echoing God's desire that we "worship the Lord in the majesty of holiness" (Psalm 29:2). Clearly the supreme duty of the creature for time and eternity is to worship the Creator.

My own heart has been relentlessly pursued by the lion of worship as over the years I have traversed the Scripture. My mind has been inescapably stalked by worship's awesome and majestic reality. History is moving along a path that will someday widen into what Isaiah calls "a highway of holiness." There "the ransomed of the Lord" forever will worship with "joyful shouting" and "everlasting joy" (Isaiah 35:8-10). In fact, how you worship now reflects the hope of your eternal destiny.

In my ministry, I have always longed to lead people to a personal encounter with the majesty of our living, holy God, yet for years I fell short of fully understanding what worship was and how it was to be accomplished. Out of recent personal frustration with my own failures in worship and a deep concern for a contemporary church that seemed to know as little as I about true worship, I sought to better understand the Bible's message that worship is the essential expression of service rendered unto God.

God has now given me the desire to pursue that stalking lion. I long to have God's people join me, but I struggle because the church often seems so pragmatic, so programmed and success-centered. In the process of striving to fulfill our needs and satisfy our desires, the church has slipped into a philosophy of "Christian humanism" that is flawed with self-love, self-esteem, self-fulfillment, and self-glory.

There appears to be scant concern about worshiping our glorious God on His terms. So-called worship seems little more than some liturgy (high or low) equated with stained-glass windows, organ music, or emotion-filled songs and prayers. If the bulletin didn't say "Worship Service," maybe we wouldn't know what we were supposed to be doing. And that reflects the absence of a worshiping life—of which a Sunday service is to be only a corporate overflow.

This book is a call to personal worship of the thrice holy God. It is a call to a radically different type of living on the part of the believer; to a way of life that seeks to worship God continually—not just on Sunday. The call is new in the sense that Christians in our time have generally missed God's emphasis. The call is old in the sense that it sounds forth again the psalmist's invitation:

Come let us worship and bow down; let us kneel before the Lord our Maker. For He is our God, and we are the people of His pasture and the sheep of His hand.

Psalm 95:6-7a

Reading this book will force you to encounter our God in all His glory. An obedient response will transform you into a true worshiper, fulfilling the ultimate priority.

Commit yourself to prayerfully learning with me, and experience as did I the life-changing truth about worship.

# 1

# What the World Needs Now

A few years ago the *Chicago Tribune* reported the story of a New Mexico woman who was frying tortillas when she noticed that the skillet burns on one of her tortillas resembled the face of Jesus. Excited, she showed it to her husband and neighbors, and they all agreed that there was a face etched on the tortilla and that it truly bore a resemblance to Jesus.

So the woman went to her priest to have the tortilla blessed. She testified that the tortilla had changed her life, and her husband agreed that she had been a more peaceful, happy, submissive wife since the tortilla had arrived. The priest, not accustomed to blessing tortillas, was somewhat reluctant but agreed to do it.

The woman took the tortilla home, put it in a glass case with piles of cotton to make it look like it was floating on clouds, built a special altar for it, and opened the little shrine to visitors. Within a few months, more than eight thousand people came to the shrine of the Jesus of the Tortilla, and all of them agreed that the face in the burn marks on the tortilla was the face of Jesus (except for one reporter who said he thought it looked like former heavyweight boxing champion Leon Spinks).

1

It seems incredible that so many people would worship a tortilla, but such a distorted concept of worship is not really unusual in contemporary society. Tragically, although the Bible is clear about how and whom and when we are to worship, little genuine worship takes place today. In fact, worship is one of the most misunderstood doctrines in all the Scriptures, and that is spiritually debilitating, because an understanding of worship is vital to any full application of Scripture.

WORSHIP IN THE BIBLE

The concept of worship dominates the Bible. In Genesis, we discover that the Fall came when man failed to worship God. In Revelation we learn that all of history culminates in an eternal worshiping community in the presence of a loving God. From the beginning in Genesis all the way through to the consummation in Revelation, the doctrine of worship is woven into the warp and woof of the biblical text.

Jesus quoted Deuteronomy 6:4-5 and called it the greatest commandment: "Hear, O Israel! The Lord our God is one Lord; and you shall love the Lord your God with all your heart, and with all your soul, and with all your mind, and with all your strength" (Mark 12:29-30). That is a call for worship, and it affirms worship as the universal priority.

Exodus 20 records the giving of the Ten Commandments. The very first of those commandments calls for and regulates worship:

> I am the Lord your God, who brought you out of the land of Egypt, out of the house of slavery. You shall have no other gods before Me. You shall not make for yourself an idol, or any likeness of what is in heaven above or on the earth beneath or in the water under the earth. You shall not worship them or serve them; for I, the Lord your God, am a jealous God. [vv. 2-5]

In the Old Testament, worship covered all of life; it was the focus of the people of God. For example, the Tabernacle was designed and laid out to emphasize the priority of worship. The description of its details requires seven chapters—243 verses—in Exodus, yet only 31 verses in Genesis are devoted to the creation of the world.

The Tabernacle was designed only for worship. It was the place where God met His people, and to use it for anything but worship would have been considered the grossest blasphemy. In the Tabernacle there were no seats—the Israelites didn't go there to attend a service, and they didn't go there for entertainment. They went there to worship God. If they had a meeting for any other purpose, they had it somewhere else.

The arrangement of the camp suggests that worship was central to all other activity. The Tabernacle was in the center, and immediately next to it were the priests, who led in the worship. A little farther out from the Tabernacle were the Levites, who were involved in service. Beyond that were all the tribes, facing toward the center, the place of worship.

All the political, social, and religious activity in Israel revolved around the law, and critical to the law was the list of ceremonial offerings described in Leviticus 1-7, all of which were acts of worship. The first offering on the list is the burnt offering, which was unique because it was completely consumed—offered totally to God. No part was shared either by the priests or by the offerer, as in other offerings.

The burnt offering was the most significant illustration of worship. In fact, the altar on which all the offerings were given was known as the altar of the burnt offering. Whenever the offerings are referred to in Scripture, the burnt offering appears at the beginning of the list, because when anyone comes to God he is to come first of all in an act of worship, where all is given to God. Thus God reinforced worship as the priority.

Moses' law spelled out exactly how the implements used in the worship services were to be made. For example, Exodus 30:34-36 gives a prescription for incense. Incense is symbolic of worship in the Scriptures, because its fragrance rises into the air as true worship rises to God. Verses 37-38 sound a warning about the incense:

And the incense which you shall make, you shall not make in the same proportions for yourselves; it shall be most holy to you. Whoever shall make any like it, to use as perfume, shall be cut off from his people.

God says, "Here is a recipe for a special perfume, emblematic of worship. This perfume is to be a unique and holy perfume. And if anyone dares to make this perfume for himself, just to smell better, I will kill him."

Clearly, there is something so unique, so holy about worship, that it is utterly apart from anything else in the human dimension. No man may take from God that which He has designed for Himself!

Our lives are to be like that perfume—holy, acceptable, fragrant—ascending to God as a sweet-smelling odor (see Romans 12:1 and 2 Corinthians 2:15). The person who uses his life for any purpose other than worship—no matter how noble that purpose may seem—is guilty of a grave sin. It is the same sin as that of an Israelite who misused the holy incense—a sin so serious that under the law it was punishable by death.

## WHEN WORSHIP IS WRONG

God repeatedly judged those who failed to worship Him properly. When the people of Israel worshiped the golden calf, God mercifully mitigated His initial righteous reaction, which would have been the utter destruction of the nation, and only slaughtered thousands of them. It stands as a graphic illustration of how God feels about false worship.

Leviticus 10 describes the ordination to the priesthood of Nadab and Abihu, the sons of Aaron the high priest. They had waited all through the years of their childhood and youth to become priests, being prepared and designed and trained for the priesthood, and now they were to be ordained.

But in their first real function as priests, they offered "strange fire." They did not do what was prescribed to be done as priests, leading the people in worship. They acted independently of the revelation of God regarding proper worship, and instantly God killed both of them.

It was a sad day. After anticipating all their lives leading the people in worship, they forfeited it all with one false move the first day. They were young men, excited, well-meaning, perhaps. But they disobeyed, and they were dead on the spot.

King Saul was guilty of a similar sin. In 1 Samuel 13:8-14, we read,

> He waited seven days, according to the appointed time set by Samuel, but Samuel did not come to Gilgal; and the people were scattering from him. So Saul said, "Bring to me the burnt offering and the peace offerings." And he offered the burnt offering. And it came about as soon as he finished offering the burnt offering, that behold, Samuel came; and Saul went out to meet him and to greet him. But Samuel said, "What have you done?" And Saul said, "Because I saw that the people were scattering from me, and that you did not come within the appointed days, and that the Philistines were assembling at Michmash, therefore I said, 'Now the Philistines will come down against me at Gilgal, and I have not asked the favor of the Lord.' So I forced myself and offered the burnt offering." And Samuel said to Saul, "You have acted foolishly; you have not kept the commandment of the Lord your God, which He commanded you, for now the Lord would have established your kingdom over Israel forever. But now your kingdom shall not endure. The Lord has sought out for Himself a man after His own heart, and the Lord has appointed him as a ruler over His people, because you have not kept what the Lord commanded you."

Saul decided to usurp the role of a priest. He departed from God's prescribed method of worship, and it ultimately cost his descendants the throne.

Uzzah was a Kohathite. The Kohathites had one task, and that was to transport the Ark of the Covenant. One of the basic principles they learned was never to touch the Ark. It was carried by poles pushed through rings, and transported on their shoulders in a manner explicitly prescribed in Numbers 4:5-6. Verse 15 says that it was to be covered carefully "so that they may not touch the holy objects and die."

That was God's method. Second Samuel 6 describes Uzzah's method:

> They placed the Ark of God on a new cart that they might bring it from the house of Abinadab which was on the hill; and Uzzah and Ahio, the sons of Abinadab, were leading the new cart. [v. 3]
> But when they came to the threshing floor of Nacon, Uzzah reached out toward the Ark of God and took hold of it, for the oxen nearly upset it. And the anger of the Lord burned against Uzzah, and God struck him down there for his irreverence; and he died there by the Ark of God. [vv. 6-7]

Uzzah, in disobedience to the divinely ordained method, was allowing the Ark to be transported on a cart, albeit a new cart. As the cart bumped along the road it almost overturned. Uzzah, trained all his life to protect the Ark of the Covenant, reached out to stop it from falling off the cart. He touched it, and God slew him on the spot.

It may seem as if Uzzah were only trying to do his job, but he was malfunctioning. He was endeavoring to carry out a responsibility before God in a way that did not fit the revelation God had given. He may have seen his act as one of worship, an attempt to preserve the holiness of God, but he defiled the Ark by the touch of his hand, and it cost him his life.

God will not accept deviant worship. Some would insist that any kind of sincere worship is acceptable to God, but that is not true. The Bible clearly teaches that those who offer self-styled worship are unacceptable to God, regardless of their good intentions. No matter how pure our motivation may seem or how sincere we are in our attempts, if we fail to worship God according to His revelation, He cannot bless us.

FOUR KINDS OF UNACCEPTABLE WORSHIP

Scripture suggests at least four categories of deviant worship. One is *the worship of false gods.* There is no other God but the God of the Bible, and He is a jealous God who will not tolerate the worship of another. In Isaiah 48:11, God says; "My glory will I not give to another." Exodus 34:14 says, "You shall not worship any other god, for the Lord, whose name is Jealous, is a jealous God."

Yet the world worships false gods. Romans 1:21 indicts all of mankind: "Even though they knew God," Paul wrote, speaking of the human race, "they did not honor Him as God, or give thanks." In fact, when they refused to worship God, they began to make images. They "exchanged the glory of the incorruptible God for an image in the form of corruptible man and of birds and fourfooted animals and crawling creatures" (v. 23).

They refused to worship God, turning instead to false gods, and that is unacceptable. Verse 24 tells the consequences of worshiping a false god: "God gave them over in the lusts of their hearts to impurity." Verse 26 says, "God gave them over to degrading passions." Verse 28 adds, "God gave them over to a depraved mind."

The result of their improper worship was that God simply gave them over to their sin and its consequences. Can you think of anything worse? Their sin increasingly became the dominating factor in their lives, and ultimately, in Romans 1:32—2:1, we learn that they faced judgment without any excuses.

Everyone worships—even an atheist. He worships himself. When men reject God they worship false gods. That, of course, is what God forbade in the first commandment.

False gods may be either material objects or mythical, supernatural beings. Material gods may be worshiped even without the conscious thought that they are deities. Job 31:24-28 says,

If I have put my confidence in gold,
And called fine gold my trust,
If I have gloated because my wealth was great,

And because my hand had secured so much;
If I have looked at the sun when it shone,
Or the moon going in splendor,
And my heart became secretly enticed,
And my hand threw a kiss from my mouth,
That too would have been an iniquity calling for
    judgment,
For I would have denied God above.

That describes a man who refuses the inclination to worship his material wealth. If you worship what you possess, if you center your life on yourself, your possessions, or even your needs, you have denied God.

Habakkuk 1:16 describes the false worship of the Chaldeans: "The Chaldeans bring all of them [the righteous] up with a hook, drag them away with their net, and gather them together in their fishing net. Therefore, they rejoice and are glad. Therefore, they offer a sacrifice to their net, and burn incense to their fishing net." "Their net" was their military might, and the god they worshiped was armed power—a false god.

Some formulate supernatural gods, supposed deities. That, too, is unacceptable. First Corinthians 10:20 says that things sacrificed to idols are really sacrificed unto demons. Therefore, if men worship false beings, they are actually worshiping the demons that impersonate those false gods.

Acts 17:29 contains a marvelous observation by Paul. "Being then the offspring of God, we ought not to think that the Divine Nature is like gold or silver or stone, an image formed by the art and thought of man." We are made in God's image, and we are not silver, stone, or wood. How could we think that our Creator would be such?

A second kind of unacceptable worship is *the worship of the true God in a wrong form*. Exodus 32:7-9 records God's response when the Israelites made a golden calf to worship:

Then the Lord spoke to Moses, "Go down at once, for your people, whom you brought up from the land of

Egypt, have corrupted themselves. They have quickly turned aside from the way which I commanded them. They have made for themselves a molten calf, and have worshiped it, and have sacrificed unto it, and said, 'This is your god, O Israel, who brought you up from the land of Egypt!' "

When the Israelites constructed the molten calf, they were worshiping the true God, but they had reduced Him to an image.

Years later, as recorded in Deuteronomy 4:14-19, Moses said to the assembled Israelites,

And the Lord commanded me at that time to teach you statutes and judgments, that you might perform them in the land where you are going over to possess it. So watch yourself carefully, since you did not see any form on the day the Lord spoke to you at Horeb from the midst of the fire. Lest you act corruptly and make a graven image for yourselves in the form of any figure, the likeness of male or female, the likeness of any winged bird that flies in the sky, the likeness of anything that creeps on the ground, the likeness of any fish that is in the water below the earth. And beware, lest you lift up your eyes to heaven and see the sun and the moon and the stars, all the host of heaven, and be drawn away and worship them and serve them, those which the Lord your God has allotted to all the peoples under the whole heaven.

In other words, when God revealed Himself to the Israelites, He was not represented in any visible form. There was no tangible representation of God—and that is true of God throughout the Scriptures. Why? Because God does not wish to be reduced to any image.

If you think of God as an old man with a beard sitting in a chair—that's unacceptable. Idolatry does not begin with a sculptor's hammer, it begins with the mind. When we think of God, what should we visualize? Absolutely nothing. No visual conception of God could properly represent His eternal glory. That may be why God is described as light. It is not possible to make a statue of light.

A third kind of deviant worship is *the worship of the true God in a self-styled manner.* As we have seen, Nadab and Abihu, Saul, and Uzzah were all guilty of worshiping God in their own way without regard to His revelation. That is false worship just as surely as worshiping a stone idol is false worship, and God does not accept it.

The Pharisees tried to worship the true God with a self-styled system, and Jesus told them, "You yourselves transgress the commandment of God for the sake of your tradition" (Matthew 15:3). Their worship was an abomination.

A far more subtle kind of false worship than any of the three we have mentioned is *the worship of the true God in the right way, with a wrong attitude.*

If we eliminate all false gods, all images of the true God, and all self-styled modes of worship, our worship will still be unacceptable if the heart attitude is not right. Perhaps you don't worship false gods or images of the true God. And maybe you are not guilty of inventing your own way to worship. But do you worship with the right attitude? If not, your worship is unacceptable to God.

Is your whole heart in worship? When it comes time to give, do you give the best of all you have? Is your inner being filled with awe and reverence? Not many can answer those questions in the affirmative.

In Malachi 1 God denounces the people of Israel for the inadequacy of their worship. "You are presenting defiled food upon My altar," He says (v. 7). They were treating the matter of worship with disdain, with flippancy. By offering blind, lame, and sick animals (v. 8) instead of bringing the best they had, they were demonstrating contempt for the seriousness of worship. In verse 10, God says, "I am not pleased with you...nor will I accept an offering from you." He declined to accept their worship, because their attitude was not right.

Amos also gives insight into the intensity of God's

hatred of worship with the wrong attitude. In Amos 5:21, God says,

I hate, I reject your festivals, nor do I delight in your solemn assemblies. Even though you offer up to Me burnt offerings and your grain offerings, I will not accept them; and I will not even look at the peace offerings of your fatlings. Take away from Me the noise of your songs; I will not even listen to the sound of your harps. But let justice roll down like waters and righteousness like an ever-flowing stream.

Hosea saw the same truth. Hosea 6:4-6 says,

What shall I do with you, O Ephraim? What shall I do with you, O Judah? For your loyalty is like a morning cloud, and like the dew which goes away early. Therefore I have hewn them in pieces by the prophets; I have slain them by the words of My mouth; and the judgments on you are like the light that goes forth. For I delight in loyalty rather than sacrifice, and in the knowledge of God rather than burnt offerings.

It was hypocrisy, not worship. The offerings were empty—like many today, they were guilty of giving God the symbol, but not the reality.
Isaiah 1 contains the same indictment:

"What are your multiplied sacrifices to Me?" says the Lord. "I have had enough of burnt offerings of rams, and the fat of fed cattle. And I take no pleasure in the blood of bulls, lambs, or goats. When you come to appear before Me, who requires of you this trampling of My courts? Bring your worthless offerings no longer, incense is an abomination to Me. New moon and sabbath, the calling of assemblies—I cannot endure iniquity and the solemn assembly. I hate your new moon festivals and your appointed feasts, they have become a burden to Me. I am weary of bearing them. So when you spread out your hands in prayer, I will hide My eyes from you, yes, even though you multiply your prayers, I will not listen." [vv. 11-15]

Read carefully the minor prophets. The prophecies of Israel's and Judah's destruction are related to the fact that they did not worship God with the proper attitude.

## OUR GREATEST NEED

Perhaps the greatest need in all of Christendom is for a clear understanding of the biblical teaching about worship. When the church fails to worship properly, it fails in every other area. And the world is suffering because of its failure.

Much of the world offers false worship, the kind of worship that focuses on a tortilla, on material things, on ritual or form, or even on divine blessings; or the kind of worship that follows a self-styled form or demonstrates a wrong attitude. God will not accept it. The Bible is explicit on that.

We must seek a fresh understanding of worship. God has commanded it. Our ministry depends on it. It is crucial to our relationship to Him and our testimony in this world. We cannot afford to ignore it. Too much is at stake.

# 2

# Worship as a Way of Life

How broad is the biblical concept of worship? And how accurate is your perception of it? Worship is to the Christian life what the mainspring is to a watch, what the engine is to a car. It is the very core, the most essential element.

Worship cannot be isolated or relegated to just one place, time, or segment of our lives. We cannot verbally thank and praise God while living lives of selfishness and carnality. That kind of effort at worship is a perversion. Real acts of worship must be the overflow of a worshiping life.

In Psalm 45:1, David says, "My heart overflows with a good theme." The Hebrew word for *overflow* means "to boil over," and in a sense that is what praise actually is. The heart is so warmed by righteousness and love that, figuratively, it reaches the boiling point. Praise is the boiling over of a hot heart. It is reminiscent of what the disciples experienced on the road to Emmaus: "Were not our hearts burning within us?" (Luke 24:36). As God warms the heart with righteousness and love, the resulting life of praise that boils over is the truest expression of worship.

13

## WHAT IS WORSHIP?

Here is a simple definition of worship: worship is honor and adoration directed to God. We need to start with no more detailed definition than that. As we study the concept of worship from the Word of God, that definition will fill up with richness.

The New Testament uses several words for worship. Two of them particularly are noteworthy. The first is *proskuneo*, a commonly used term that literally means "to kiss toward," "to kiss the hand," or "to bow down." It is the word for worship used to signify humble adoration. The second word is *latreuo*, which suggests rendering honor, or paying homage.

Both terms carry the idea of giving, because worship *is* giving something to God. The Anglo-Saxon word from which we get our English word is *weorthscipe*, which is tied to the concept of worthiness. Worship is ascribing to God His worth, or stating and affirming His supreme value.

When we talk about worship, we are talking about something *we* give to God. Modern Christianity seems committed instead to the idea that God should be giving to us. God *does* give to us abundantly, but we need to understand the balance of that truth—we are to render honor and adoration to God. That consuming, selfless desire to give to God is the essence and the heart of worship. It begins with the giving first of ourselves, and then of our attitudes, and then of our possessions—until worship is a way of life.

### WORSHIP IN THREE DIMENSIONS

A key adjective, often used in the New Testament to describe proper acts of worship, is the word *acceptable*. Every worshiper seeks to offer that which is acceptable, and at least three categories of acceptable worship are specified in Scripture.

*The outward dimension.* First, worship can be reflected in how we behave toward others. Romans 14:18 says, "For he who in this way serves [*latreuo*] Christ is acceptable to God." What is this acceptable offering given to God? The context reveals that it is being sensitive to a weaker brother. Verse 13 says, "Therefore let us not judge one another anymore, but rather determine this—not to put an obstacle or a stumbling block in a brother's way." In other words, when we treat fellow Christians with the proper kind of sensitivity, that is an acceptable act of worship. It honors God, who created and loves that person, and it reflects God's compassion and care.

Romans 15:16 implies that evangelism is a form of acceptable worship. Paul writes that special grace was given to him "to be a minister of Christ Jesus to the Gentiles, ministering as a priest the gospel of God, that my offering of the Gentiles might become acceptable." The Gentiles who were won to Jesus Christ by his ministry became an offering of worship to God. In addition, they who were won became worshipers themselves.

In Philippians 4:18, Paul thanks the Philippians for a gift of money to help him in his ministry: "I have received everything in full, and have an abundance; I am amply supplied, having received from Epaphroditus what you have sent, a fragrant aroma, an acceptable sacrifice, well-pleasing to God." Here, acceptable worship is described as giving to those in need. That glorifies God by demonstrating His love.

So worship can be expressed by sharing love with fellow believers, sharing the gospel with unbelievers, and meeting the needs of people on a very physical level. We can sum it up in a single word: acceptable worship is *giving*. It is a love that shares.

*The inward dimension.* A second category of worship involves our personal behavior. Ephesians 5:8-10 says, "Walk as children of light (for the fruit of the light consists in all goodness and righteousness and truth), trying to learn what is pleasing to the Lord." The word *pleasing* is from a Greek word that means "acceptable." In this context, he is referring to goodness, righteousness, and truth, saying clearly that to do good is an acceptable act of worship toward God.

Paul begins 1 Timothy 2 by urging Christians to pray for those in authority in order that believers may live tranquil lives in godliness and dignity. Note carefully that the final words in verse 2 are "godliness and dignity." Verse 3 goes on to say, "This is good and acceptable in the sight of God our Savior."

So sharing is an act of worship, and that is the effect of worship on others. Doing good is also an act of worship, and that is its effect in our own lives. There is one other relationship that is affected by our worship—our relationship with God.

*The upward dimension.* This third category, which marvelously sums up worship, is described in Hebrews 13:15-16. Verse 15 says, "Through Him, then, let us continually offer up a sacrifice of praise to God, that is, the fruit of lips that give thanks to His name." As we look at worship in its Godward focus, we discover that it is thanksgiving and praise. With verse 16, the passage brings together all three categories of worship: "And do not neglect doing good and sharing; for with such sacrifices God is pleased."

Praising God, doing good, and sharing with others—all legitimate, scriptural acts of worship. That draws into the concept of worship every activity and relationship of human living. The implication is that just as the Scriptures are dedicated to the subject of worship from cover to cover, so the believer should be dedicated to the activity of worship, consumed with a desire to use every moment of his life to devote himself to doing good, sharing, and praising God.

WHOLE-LIFE WORSHIP

Our definition of worship is enriched when we understand that true worship touches each area of life. We are to honor and adore God in everything.

Paul makes a powerful statement in Romans 12:1-2 about the concept of whole-life worship. His words there come after what is possibly the greatest exposition of theology in all of Scripture. Those first eleven chapters of Romans are a monumental treatise, taking us from the wrath of God through the redemption of man, to the plan of God for Israel and the church. All the great themes of redemptive theology are there, and in response to them we find the very familiar words of Romans 12:1-2:

> I urge you therefore, brethren, by the mercies of God, to present your bodies a living and holy sacrifice, acceptable to God, which is your spiritual service of worship. And do not be conformed to this world, but be transformed by the renewing of your mind, that you may prove what the will of God is, that which is good and acceptable and perfect.

*The mercies of God* refers to what Paul has described in the first eleven chapters. The theme of those chapters is God's merciful work on our behalf. Through eleven chapters of doctrine, Paul defines the Christian life and all its benefits. Now he says that our only adequate response to what God has done for us, and the starting point for acceptable, spiritual worship, is to present ourselves as a living sacrifice.

First Peter reiterates the same basic truth. In chapter 1, Peter gives a full and rich statement of what Christ has done for us:

> May grace and peace be yours in fullest measure. Blessed be the God and Father of our Lord Jesus Christ, who according to His great mercy has caused us to be born again to a living hope through the resurrection of Jesus Christ from the dead, to obtain an inheritance which is imperishable and undefiled and will not fade away, reserved in heaven for you, who are protected by the power of God through faith for a salvation ready to be revealed in the last time. [1 Peter 1:2a-5]

Note our response to that in chapter 2, verse 5: "You also, as living stones, are being built up as a spiritual house for a holy priesthood, to offer up spiritual sacrifices acceptable to God through Jesus Christ." Peter's argument is identical to Paul's: because of what God has done for us, we are to be occupied with offering up acceptable spiritual sacrifices of worship.

Another New Testament passage that parallels
Romans 12:1-2 is Hebrews 12:28-29. Verse 28 says,
"Therefore, since we receive a kingdom which cannot be
shaken [again he is dealing with what God has done for
us], let us show gratitude, by which we may offer [the
word is a form of *latreuo*] to God an acceptable service
with reverence and awe." Our all-inclusive response to
God, our chief priority and the only activity that matters,
is pure, acceptable worship.

## THE ORDER OF PRIORITIES

God's Word repeatedly confirms the absolute priority
of worship. Hebrews 11 contains a list of Old Testament
heroes of faith. First on the list is Abel. His life echoes one
word: *worship*. The single dominant issue in Abel's story
is that he was a true worshiper; he worshiped according
to God's will, and his offering was accepted by God. That
is really all we know about his life.

The second person in Hebrews 11 is Enoch, who also
may be identified with a single word: *walk*. Enoch
walked with God; he lived a godly, faithful, dedicated
life. One day he walked from earth to heaven!

Third on the list is Noah. When we think of Noah, the
word we think of is *work*. He spent 120 years building
the ark. That is work—the work of faith.

There is an order to Hebrews 11 that goes beyond the
chronological. It is an order of priorities: first comes worship, then walk, then work. It is the same order we saw
in the layout of the camp of Israel around the Tabernacle.
The priests, those whose function was to lead the people
in worship, camped immediately surrounding the Tabernacle. Beyond them were the Levites, whose function was
service. The positions illustrated that worship was to be
the central activity, and service was secondary.

The same order was built into the Law. Moses established specific age requirements for different ministries.
According to Numbers 1:3, a young Israelite could serve
as a soldier when he was twenty. Numbers 8:24 tells us
that a Levite could begin to work in the Tabernacle when
he was twenty-five. But Numbers 4:3 says that to be a

priest and lead the people in worship, a man had to be thirty. The reason is simple: leading in worship demands the highest level of maturity, because as the first priority in the divine order, worship holds the greatest significance.

We see the same order of priority in the activities of the angels. In Isaiah 6, the prophet describes his vision:

> In the year of king Uzziah's death, I saw the Lord, sitting on a throne, lofty and exalted, with the train of His robe filling the temple. Seraphim stood above Him, each having six wings; with two he covered his face, and with two he covered his feet, and with two he flew. And one called out to another and said, "Holy, Holy, Holy, is the Lord of Hosts, the whole earth is full of His glory." [vv. 1-3]

The seraphim are a class of angelic beings associated with the presence of God. It is particularly interesting to note that of their six wings, four are related to worship and only two are related to service. They cover their feet to protect the holiness of God. They cover their faces because they cannot look upon His glory. With the two remaining wings they are able to fly and take care of whatever activities their service requires.

Ministry must be kept in perspective. A. P. Gibbs correctly observed that ministry is that which comes down from the Father by the Son in the power of the Spirit through the human instrument. Worship starts in the human instrument and goes up by the power of the Holy Spirit through the Son to the Father.[1]

In the Old Testament, the prophet, who was a minister of God's Word, spoke from God to the people. The priest, who led the worship, spoke from the people to God. Worship is the perfect balance to ministry, but the order of priority begins with worship, not ministry.

Luke 10 tells the familiar account of Jesus' visit to Mary and Martha:

1. A.P. Gibbs, *Worship* (Kansas City: Walterick), p. 13.

Now as they were traveling along, He entered a certain village; and a woman named Martha welcomed Him into her home. And she had a sister called Mary, who moreover was listening to the Lord's word, seated at His feet. But Martha was distracted with all her preparations; and she came up to Him, and said, "Lord, do You not care that my sister has left me to do all the serving alone? Then tell her to help me." But the Lord answered and said to her, "Martha, Martha, you are worried and bothered about so many things; but only a few things are necessary, really only one, for Mary has chosen the good part, which shall not be taken away from her." [vv. 38-42]

Worship is the primary essential, and service is a wonderful and necessary corollary to it. Worship is central in the will of God—the great sine qua non of all Christian experience.

Jesus taught a similar lesson, again at the home of Mary and Martha. Lazarus, their brother, whom Jesus had raised from the dead, was there.

So they made Him a supper there, and Martha was serving; but Lazarus was one of those reclining at the table with Him. Mary therefore took a pound of very costly perfume of pure nard, and anointed the feet of Jesus, and wiped His feet with her hair; and the house was filled with the fragrance of the perfume. But Judas Iscariot, one of His disciples, who was intending to betray Him, said, "Why was this perfume not sold for three hundred denarii, and given to poor people?" Now he said this, not because he was concerned about the poor, but because he was a thief, and as he had the money box, he used to pilfer what was put into it. Jesus therefore said, "Let her alone, in order that she may keep it for the day of my burial. For the poor you always have with you, but you do not always have Me." [vv. 2-8]

What Mary did was a very humiliating thing. A woman's hair is her glory; and a man's feet, dirty with the dust or mud of the roads, are nobody's glory. To use such costly ointment (worth a year's wages) seemed incredibly wasteful to the pragmatists. Notice that they were represented by Judas. Jesus rebuked them for their attitude. Mary's act was sincere worship, and Jesus commended her for understanding the priority.

## HOW ARE WE DOING?

Tragically, the element of worship is largely missing amid all the activity that goes on in the church! A number of years ago I read a newspaper account of a christening party in a wealthy Boston suburb. The parents had opened their palatial home to friends and relatives, who had come to celebrate the wonderful event. As the party was moving along and the people were having a wonderful time eating and drinking and celebrating and enjoying one another, somebody said, "By the way, where is the baby?"

The heart of that mother jumped, and she instantly left the room and rushed into the master bedroom, where she had left the baby asleep in the middle of the massive bed. The baby was dead, smothered by the coats of the guests.

I've often thought about that in reference to how the Lord Jesus Christ is treated in His own church. We are busy supposedly celebrating Him, while He is smothered by the coats of the guests.

We have many activities and little worship. We are big on ministry and small on adoration. We are disastrously pragmatic. All we want to know about is what works. We want formulas and gimmicks, and somehow in the process, we leave out that to which God has called us.

We are too many Marthas and too few Marys. We are so deeply entrenched in the doing that we miss the being. We are programmed and informed and planned and busy, and we slight worship! We have our functionaries, our promotions, our objectives, our success-driven, numbers-conscious, traditionalistic, even faddish efforts. But too often acceptable, true, spiritual worship eludes us.

Years ago, A. W. Tozer called worship "the missing jewel of the church." If he were still with us I'm sure he would reiterate that statement without question. Three hundred fifty thousand churches in America own eighty billion dollars worth of facilities dedicated to worshiping God. But how much true worship takes place?

A distinguished explorer was making a trek in the Amazon jungle. Native tribesmen were bearing his great burdens, and he was driving them with great force to cover a lot of ground rapidly. At the end of the third day they rested, and when morning came and it was time to embark again, the natives sat on the ground by their burdens. The explorer did everything he could to get them up and moving, but they wouldn't budge. Finally, the chief said to him, "My friend, they are resting until their souls catch up to their bodies."

I wish that were happening in the church.

Worship as the Word of God presents it is internal, sacrificial, active, and productive. That is not at all like the world's concept of worship, yet it is the only kind of worship God recognizes. It is the purest kind of worship—the kind that ascends to God as sweet incense, the kind that is expressed continuously in every aspect of our lives by sharing with others, doing good works, and offering praise to God. That is the kind of worship God desires. It is worship in its deepest, most spiritual sense.

# 3

# Saved to Worship

Worship is not optional. In Matthew 4:10, in response to Satan's temptation, Jesus quoted Deuteronomy 6:13: "You shall worship the Lord your God, and serve Him only." In saying that to Satan, He swept into the command every being ever created. All are responsible to worship God.

The foundation upon which true worship is based is redemption. The Father and Son have sought to redeem us that we may become worshipers. Jesus said that the Son of Man came into the world to seek and to save that which was lost (Luke 19:10). In John 4 He reveals the purpose for His seeking: "For such people the Father seeks to be His worshipers" (v. 23). The Father sent Christ to seek and save for the specific purpose of producing worshiping people.

Thus, the objective of redemption is making worshipers. The primary reason we are redeemed is not so that we may escape hell—that is a blessed benefit, but not the major purpose. The central objective for which we are redeemed is not even so that we might enjoy the manifold eternal blessings of God. In fact, the supreme motive in our redemption is not for *us* to receive anything. Rather,

we have been redeemed so that God may receive worship—so that our lives might glorify Him. Any personal
blessing for us is a divine response to the fulfillment of
that supreme purpose.

Paul affirmed that when he described his purpose of
evangelism in Romans 1:5: "[We preach] obedience of
faith among all the Gentiles *for His name's sake*"
(emphasis added). John echoes that in 3 John 7. He
writes that missionaries were sent out to proclaim the
gospel "for the sake of the Name." Our salvation is first
of all for God's benefit.

That does not mean there is no blessing in salvation for
the believer. There is much. And there is a place for hold-
ing onto the hem of His garment and refusing to let go
until He blesses us. But the blessings are an additional
benefit—not the ultimate purpose. We are to seek to glorify God before we seek to gain anything from Him.

To be concerned primarily with the blessings is to
experience salvation in a shallow, self-centered manner.
Jesus rebuked such an attitude in Matthew 6:33, when
He said, "But seek first His kingdom and His righteousness; and all these things shall be added to you."

Throughout the Scriptures we find confirmation of this
basic truth that God's primary activity has always been
the seeking of true worshipers. From God's Word we see
that all of history consummates in heaven, where the
whole of that eternal domain of the redeemed resounds
with worship. The sole purpose of our being in heaven is
that we might worship God rightly and forever. We,
along with the redeemed of all ages, are saved to that glorious and unending end.

As It Was in the Beginning

In eternity past, before men were created, before the
earth was formed, worship was taking place. Referring to
the angels, Nehemiah 9:6 says, "The heavenly host bows
down before Thee." That is their present activity, and it
has been their activity from their creation.

When Adam and Eve were created and put in this
world they, too, worshiped God. They walked and talked

with God in the garden. They obeyed Him with unquestioning loyalty. Sin came because they abandoned pure worship by obeying Satan's advice over God's clear commandment. Their unqualified obedience to God was broken. As soon as they honored Satan's word above God's, they ceased worshiping God and were cursed (Genesis 3:1-6).

The first recorded division among men came between Cain and Abel, and the conflict had to do with the way they worshiped. Cain brought an unacceptable offering to God, and Abel brought an acceptable offering. Cain was jealous of his brother's acceptance with God, so he killed him (Genesis 4:3-8).

REDEMPTION IN THE OLD TESTAMENT

It was clear in Old Testament times that people were redeemed to worship. The exodus of Israel from Egypt is the great Old Testament illustration of redemption. After their deliverance from Egypt, the entire nation wandered for forty years in the Sinai desert until a whole generation died—and it was all because they failed to worship God properly in response to their redemption. They chose to follow their own way rather than God's, and it proved to be the way of death. That generation, including Moses, was guilty of rebellion, and they were kept out of the Promised Land.

Before the next generation finally entered the land, Moses gave them instructions for the feast of the first fruits, which was to be a reminder to them of the importance of true, acceptable worship as the response to God's redemption. Deuteronomy 26:8-9 records the words to be used in the ritual: "The Lord brought us out of Egypt with a mighty hand and an outstretched arm and with great terror and with signs and wonders; and He has brought us to this place, and has given us this land, a land flowing with milk and honey." It was a proclamation stating that God had redeemed them. Notice in verse 10 the response to that: "And you shall set [the first produce of the ground] down before the Lord your God, and worship before the Lord your God." Once the Israelites had entered the land, they had only to follow a simple formula to be guaranteed God's blessing: worship God acceptably.

Nehemiah records a great revival that took place under Ezra's ministry. The people repented, fasted, prayed, confessed their sins, and worshiped God together. A day was spent publicly reading the Word of God and confessing sin. During that revival, the Levites led the public worship by reciting all that God had done for the nation throughout its history. Nehemiah 9 is a record of their account of the times of blessing as well as the times of chastening. A distinct pattern emerged in Israel's history as the Levites saw it. Invariably when the people were worshiping God properly, God blessed them. But when they failed to worship God as He wanted to be worshiped, they were punished.

WORSHIP AND THE CROSS OF CHRIST

The life and work of Jesus Christ are inextricably linked with worship. During His earthly ministry He taught by example and command the importance of true worship. Even His death was a lesson in the meaning and significance of worship.

The twenty-second psalm is a wonderful prophetic look at the crucifixion of Christ, beginning with that familiar statement the Lord uttered on the cross, "My God, My God, why hast Thou forsaken me?" The psalm contains several prophecies that were fulfilled in our Lord's dying:

> But I am a worm, and not a man,
> A reproach of men, and despised by the people.
> All who see me sneer at me;
> They separate the lip, they wag the head, saying
> "Commit yourself to the Lord; let Him deliver him;
> Let Him rescue him, because He delights in him."
>                                    vv. 6-8
>
>> They open wide their mouth at me,
>> As a ravening and a roaring lion.
>> I am poured out like water,
>> And all my bones are out of joint;

My heart is like wax;
It is melted within me.
My strength is dried up like a potsherd,
And my tongue cleaves to my jaws;
And thou dost lay me in the dust of death.
For dogs have surrounded me;
A band of evildoers has encompassed me;
They pierced my hands and my feet.
I can count all my bones.
They look, they stare at me;
They divide my garments among them,
And for my clothing they cast lots.

vv. 13-18

To what end did Christ die? For what purpose? In verse 22 we see a turn in the text:

I will tell of Thy name to my brethren;
In the midst of the assembly I will praise Thee.
You who fear the Lord, praise Him;
All you descendants of Jacob, glorify Him;
And stand in awe of Him, all you descendants of
   Israel.

vv. 22-23

What is the right response to the death of Christ on our behalf? It is praise. It is glory. It is holy awe. The psalmist continues:

From Thee comes my praise in the great assembly;
I shall pay my vows before those who fear Him.
The afflicted shall eat and be satisfied;
Those who seek Him will praise the Lord.
Let your heart live forever!
All the ends of the earth will remember and turn to
   the Lord,
And all the families of the nations will worship before
   Thee.

vv. 25-27

Worship, then, is the essence of the matter. The proper response—the only righteous response—to the saving

death of Christ, is the heartfelt expression of true
worship.

## The Response to the Messiah

A look at the end of Isaiah's prophecy in chapter 66 as
he sees the great fruit of the Messiah's work reveals the
same perspective. He says in verse 22, " 'For just as the
new heavens and the new earth which I make will endure
before Me,' declares the Lord, 'so your offspring and your
name will endure.' " That is a promise of redemption.

In the next verse, as he looks ahead to the new heaven
and the new earth, Isaiah writes: "And it shall come to
pass, that from one moon to another, and from one sabbath to another, shall all flesh come to worship before
me, saith the Lord" (KJV*). That is the goal and the consummation of the Messiah's work. Worship!

Shift your thinking to the New Testament. The Messiah
arrived, and the overwhelming response to Him was worship. Matthew traces it in a most marvelous way.

The response of the wise men—the initial response to
Christ—was worship. "And they came into the house
and saw the Child with Mary His mother; and they fell
down and worshipped Him" (Matthew 2:11).

In Matthew 8 we find a very moving incident. "And
behold, there came a leper *and worshipped him*, saying,
Lord, if thou wilt, thou canst make me clean" (v. 2, KJV,
emphasis added). Those to whom He ministered worshiped. Even the sick and blind and lame responded to
Him with praise and adoration.

In Matthew 9:18, Jesus was speaking of the wonderful
reality of the New Covenant: "While he spake these
things unto them, behold, there came a certain ruler, *and
worshipped him*, saying, My daughter is even now dead:
but come and lay thy hand upon her, and she shall live"
(KJV, emphasis added).

In chapter 14 we find Jesus with His disciples. He has
walked on the water, He has calmed their hearts, the
wind has ceased, "and those who were in the boat wor-

---

* King James Version.

shiped him, saying, 'You are certainly God's Son!' " (v. 33).

Matthew 15:25 (KJV) tells of a woman of Canaan who "worshipped Him, saying, Lord, help me."

In His last days here on earth, our Lord went into a mountain with His disciples. In one of the final verses of his gospel Matthew writes, "And when they saw Him, they worshiped Him" (28:17).

Of course, not all those incidents illustrate pure, acceptable worship, but that brief survey from Matthew is representative of the normal reaction to Christ. Whether acceptably or not, people worshiped Him.

John's gospel also has the theme of worship throughout its chapters. John 2 tells of Jesus' entry into Jerusalem. He came first to the Temple, made a whip, and cleansed the Temple. Why did He do that? Because God sent Jesus Christ into the world to bring into His presence true worshipers. And one of His first acts was to throw out the false ones.

In chapter 3 we meet the first of the true worshipers in John's gospel—Nicodemus. In chapter 4, Jesus tells the woman at the well that the Father seeks true worshipers.

WORSHIP WITHOUT END

You could follow the theme all the way through the New Testament to the book of Revelation, where we find eternal universal worship of God. In the vision of the end times that he describes throughout the book, John repeatedly focuses on acts of worship that occur, and we can infer that they left a profound impression on the apostle.

In Revelation 5:13-14 he wrote,

And every created thing which is in heaven and on the earth and under the earth and on the sea, and all things in them, I heard saying, "To Him who sits on the throne, and to the Lamb, be blessing and honor and glory and dominion forever and ever." And the four living creatures kept saying, "Amen." And the elders fell down and worshiped.

He wrote,

> And the seventh angel sounded; and there arose loud
> voices in heaven, saying, "The kingdom of the world
> has become the kingdom of our Lord, and of His Christ;
> and He will reign forever and ever." And the twenty-
> four elders, who sit on their thrones before God, fell on
> their faces and worshiped God, saying, "We give Thee
> thanks, O Lord God, the Almighty." [11:15-17]

> And I saw another angel flying in midheaven, having
> an eternal gospel to preach to those who live on the
> earth, and to every nation and tribe and tongue and
> people; and he said with a loud voice, "Fear God, and
> give Him glory, because the hour of His judgment has
> come; and worship Him who made the heaven and the
> earth and sea and springs of waters." [14:6-7]

Notice that the angel's message is called "the eternal gospel." What is the eternal message? "Fear God, and give
Him glory . . . and worship Him who made the heaven
and the earth."

John also records the words of the multitude who had
been victorious over the beast:

> Who will not fear, O Lord, and glorify Thy name? For
> Thou alone art holy; for all the nations will come and
> worship before Thee. [15:4]

And the behavior of the elders and living creatures: "And
the twenty-four elders and the four living creatures fell
down and worshiped God who sits on the throne saying,
'Amen; Hallelujah!' " (19:4).

Then John relates a personal incident that happened:
"I fell at his [the angel's] feet to worship him. And he said
to me, 'Do not do that; I am a fellow servant of yours and
your brethren who hold the testimony of Jesus; worship
God' "(19:10). Later in his vision, John again was so
amazed that he fell down to worship the angel, and he
got the same response. The angel said, "Do not do that; I
am a fellow servant of yours and of your brethren the

prophets and of those who heed the words of this book;
worship God" (22:9).

Worship God. That is the everlasting gospel, the
message that God has given from eternity to eternity. It is
the theme of Scripture, the theme of eternity, the theme of
redemptive history—to worship the true and living and
glorious God. Before the creation, after the creation, in
eternity past, in eternity future, and throughout all time
in between, worship is the theme, the central issue in all
of creation.

WHO MAY ENTER HIS HOLY HILL?

Psalm 24:3-6 gives us what is perhaps the most lovely
Old Testament picture of an acceptable worshiper:

> Who may ascend into the hill of the Lord?
> And who may stand in His holy place?
> He who has clean hands and a pure heart,
> Who has not lifted up his soul unto falsehood,
> And has not sworn deceitfully.
> He shall receive a blessing from the Lord
> And righteousness from the God of his salvation.
> This is the generation of those who seek Him,
> Who seek Thy face—even Jacob.

Who has a right to go into God's presence? Who has a
right to draw near? Those who seek Him with clean
hands and a pure heart; that is, those who worship God
acceptably. And who are those who worship God acceptably? Those who receive righteousness from God, or
those who are redeemed. The two characteristics are
inseparable. One does not become a true worshiper apart
from redemption, and one who is genuinely redeemed
becomes a true worshiper. He is done with superficial
religion and false gods and adores the living and true
God.

So how you worship reveals your destiny because it
manifests whether the life of God is within you and
reflects whether you are acceptable to God. Those who
are acceptable have clean hands. That is, they live in
obedience to God—they have been purified and made

clean. They have pure hearts; their motives, their desires, are right. They're blessed because they are the generation who truly seek God (v. 6).

We will fail often, and at times our worship will be less than it should be, but we will pursue glory for God as those committed and recreated to worship Him. No believer is satisfied to offer worship that falls short of what God wants it to be.

On the other hand, those who refuse to worship God acceptably suffer eternal separation from His presence. In Romans 1, when God indicts the pagans of the world for their unbelief, the essence of the condemnation is that they did not properly worship God. Read what Paul wrote:

> For the wrath of God is revealed from heaven against all ungodliness and unrighteousness of men, who suppress the truth in unrighteousness, because that which may be known about God is evident within them; for God made it evident to them. For since the creation of the world His invisible attributes, His eternal power and divine nature, have been clearly seen, being understood through what has been made, so that they are without excuse. For even though they knew God, *they did not honor Him as God, or give thanks;* but they became futile in their speculations, and their foolish heart was darkened. [vv. 18-21, emphasis added]

There, in a very simple statement, is the sum of God's attitude toward sinful man. Man's condemnation, Paul says, can be traced to his failure to honor God as God. If worship is the ultimate priority, not to worship is the ultimate affront to God. And a refusal to worship God properly is the heart of the issue of mankind's lostness.

## Turning Pagans into Worshipers

Unacceptable worship has eternally disastrous consequences, because God cannot accept one whose worship is unacceptable. Conversely, true worshipers experience God's eternal blessing, and it is to that end that God saves us. Redemption can be viewed, then, as the transformation of the false worshiper into a true worshiper. If you're truly saved, you're an acceptable worshiper. If you're an acceptable worshiper you've come into God's presence. Thus, as you examine your worship you can understand whether or not you're saved. Worship becomes a test of the genuineness of salvation.

In John 4, Jesus uses the term *true worshipers* to describe all believers. *True worshiper* is equivalent to *Christian*, or *believer*, or *saint*, or *child of God*, or any other term used to describe our union with Christ. It is perhaps a more appropriate description, however, because it expresses the result of salvation in active, rather than static, terminology.

We are true worshipers who worship the Father in spirit and in truth. As believers, we may not always worship as fully and as consistently as we ought to, but nevertheless, we are true worshipers. In fact, acceptable worship is our chief distinguishing characteristic.

A look at 1 Corinthians 14 will help our thinking at this point. Paul wrote to the believers in Corinth about the importance of order in their services, speaking out against the excesses of the Corinthian assembly, particularly regarding tongues and spiritual gifts. He rebuked them for the chaos and confusion that was occurring in their assembly:

> If therefore the whole church should assemble together and all speak in tongues, and ungifted men or unbelievers enter, will they not say that you are mad? But if all prophesy, and an unbeliever or ungifted man enters, he is convicted by all, he is called to account by all; the secrets of his heart are disclosed; and so he will fall on his face and worship God, declaring that God is certainly among you. [vv. 23-25]

In other words, if you want to really crack open someone's heart, if you really want him to believe and desire to experience God's presence and transforming power, the best approach is not speaking in tongues. Rather, speak so he can understand—speak that which will convict him, condemn him, and reveal his heart to him. When he is reached, his response will be worship: "He

will fall on his face and worship God." Salvation will
produce a worshiper.

## THE MARK OF THE BELIEVER

Philippians 3:3 contains what may be the best definition of a Christian anywhere in the Bible: "For we are the
true circumcision, *who worship in the Spirit of God and
glory in Christ Jesus and put no confidence in the
flesh*" (emphasis added).

What does Paul mean by that? He is contrasting the
Christian with the Judaizer, who taught that the mark of
the believer was a physical mark—circumcision. Paul
says we have, rather, a spiritual mark. A Jew is identified by physical circumcision. But if you want to identify
Christians what do you use? Here is our mark. Here is
how we are distinguished: "[We] worship God in the
spirit, and rejoice in Christ Jesus, and have no confidence in the flesh" (KJV).

In spite of what has been written, the true mark of the
Christian is not love. The mark of the Christian is that he
truly worships God in the spirit. All virtues flow from
that.

## HOW ABOUT YOU?

A Christian is a worshiper of God. He is not as preoccu-
pied with what he gets as with what he gives. He is not
just seeking a blessing. He is offering to God a sacrifice—
the sacrifice of sharing, of doing righteously, and of
praise. The basis for worship, the key that unlocks the
door and makes worship possible, that which transforms
an unacceptable worshiper into an acceptable worshiper,
is salvation.

If you are redeemed and you aren't now worshiping
acceptably, you deny that very thing for which you were
redeemed. Face the questions: Do you worship God? Is it
a way of life for you? Scripture calls for worship; destiny
calls for worship; eternity calls for worship; the angels
call for worship. Our Lord commands it. Are you a true
worshiper? As a true worshiper, is your worship all it
should be?

# 4

# God: Is He? Who Is He?

Acceptable worship demands that God be known—worship cannot occur where the true God is not believed in, adored, and obeyed. The object of our worship must be right if our worship is to be acceptable. We must consider the God we worship.

Paul's experience with the religious philosophers on Mars Hill in Acts 17 brought him into a classic confrontation with a case of unacceptable worship. The Greeks had an idol to "the unknown god." Paul used that idol as a starting point to preach to them about worshiping the true God. Paul, in essence, told them, "You are worshiping in ignorance. Let me tell you about this unknown God. He can be known. It does no good at all to guess about who He is or how to worship Him."

God has so clearly revealed Himself to us in His Word and through His Son that man is without excuse if he persists in unbelief. Faith, then, and more specifically, faith in God as He has revealed Himself to us, is the fundamental requirement for true worship. Hebrews 11:6 says,

But without faith it is impossible to please Him,

for he who comes to God must believe that He is, and that He is a rewarder of those who seek Him.

That verse states two facts about God—that He exists, and that it is possible to know something of His nature. It suggests that the true worshiper must have those two issues settled in his mind.

Historian Will Durant said, "The greatest question of our time is not Communism versus individualism. It is not Europe versus America. It is not even the east versus the west. It is whether man can bear to live without God." I agree. The major issue in the world is the reality of God.

## DID MAN CREATE GOD?

Skeptics say that Christians have simply invented God. Religion, they claim, has devised supernatural explanations for what men do not understand, and there really is no supernatural reality—God is a human creation.

Sigmund Freud, for example, said that man made God. That, of course, is the reversal of what the Bible says, that God created man. Freud said in his book *The Future of an Illusion* that because man desperately needs security; because he has deep-seated fears; and because he lives in a threatening world in which he has very little control over his circumstances, he invented God to meet his psychological needs. Man feels the need for an invisible means of support, but there is no God except in man's imagination.

That idea was spawned out of a corrupt mind. It is totally indefensible, and yet there have been myriads of people who have believed it. It demonstrates a simplistic, ignorant view of the world's religions. When man manufactures a god it rarely is a saving, delivering god. The gods invented by man don't become psychologically supportive of man, but are oppressive gods who continually have to be appeased. When a woman in India throws her baby into the Ganges River to drown in hopes of appeasing some god, she does not see that god as someone to deliver her from her problems. Her god is a fearful ogre. Indeed, false gods are man's invention, but they are not like the true God, and in no way do they negate the reality of the true God.

Man has not made God—in fact, if man had his way he would prefer that the God of the Bible did not exist. Unregenerate man is God's would-be murderer. He does his best to eliminate the true God. He invents false gods. He postulates theology that says God is dead. He devises philosophies and life-styles that assert that the very idea of a God is ludicrous.

The majority of people deny God's existence one way or the other. Many who are not philosophical atheists are pragmatic atheists. Although they do not reject the concept of God, they live as if He didn't exist. Titus 1:16 describes such people: "They profess to know God, but by their deeds they deny Him, being detestable and disobedient, and worthless for any good deed."

That has been the norm since Adam and Eve. Immediately after they sinned, they hid themselves from God. They tried to act as if God didn't exist, and mankind has followed their pattern throughout history. Romans 1 tells us that men know in their hearts God exists. Verse 19 says, "That which is known about God is evident in them." Verse 20 says, "Since the creation of the world His invisible attributes, His eternal power and divine nature, have been clearly seen." Verse 21 says, "They knew God." And verse 28 says, "They did not see fit to acknowledge God."

Freud is wrong. Man has not invented God. Man does not wish God into existence. Man would wish God out of existence, if he had his way.

## How Can We Be Sure of God?

The Bible presupposes, rather than proves, God's existence. Scripture says this about God in Psalm 90:2: "Before the mountains were born, or Thou didst give birth to the earth and the world, even from everlasting to everlasting, Thou art God." That is a classic doctrinal affirmation about God. It tells us that God is the only

God: "Thou art God." It tells us that God is the eternal
God: "From everlasting to everlasting, Thou art God." It
tells us that God is the Creator God: "Thou didst give
birth to the earth and the world."

As Christians we accept one foundational truth—
God—and everything else makes sense. An atheist denies
God and has to accept incredible explanations for everything else. It takes more faith to deny God than to believe
in Him.

Theologians give several arguments for the existence of
God. Logic can't prove God's existence, but it clearly
show us that there is more reason to believe in God than
there is *not* to believe in Him.

One logical reason to accept the existence of God is the
*teleological argument*. That comes from the Greek word
*teleos*, which means "perfect result," "end," or "finish."
Something that is completed and perfected shows evidence of a maker. Design implies a designer. Take your
watch apart and put all the pieces in your pocket. You
will shake your leg a long time before you will ever hear
the watch tick. When something works, someone made it
work. If you see a piano you don't assume that an ele-
phant ran into a tree where someone was sitting on a
branch playing a harp, and all the ivory, wood, and
strings fell together and became a piano. The teleological
argument says that the order in the universe is evidence
that a supreme intelligence, God, created it.

A second argument for God is the *aesthetic argument*.
It claims that because there is beauty and truth there has
to be somewhere in the universe a standard on which
beauty and truth are based.

The *volitional argument* says that because man faces
a myriad of choices and has the ability to make willful
decisions, there must be somewhere an infinite will, and
the world must be the expression of that will.

The *moral argument* says that the very fact we know
there is right and wrong suggests the necessity of an
absolute standard. If anything is right and anything is
wrong, somewhere there is Someone who determines
which is which.

The *cosmological argument* is the argument of cause and effect. It concludes that someone made the universe, because every effect must be traceable to a cause. The cause of infinity must be infinite. The cause of endless time must be eternal. The cause of power must be omnipotent. The cause of limitless space must be omnipresent. The cause of knowledge must be omniscient. The cause of personality must be personal. The cause of feeling must be emotional. The cause of will must be volitional. The cause of ethical values must be moral. The cause of spiritual values must be spiritual. The cause of beauty must be aesthetic. The cause of righteousness must be holy. The cause of justice must be just. The cause of love must be loving. The cause of life must be living.

Psalm 14:1 and Psalm 53:1 say, "The fool has said in his heart, 'There is no God.' " Only a fool would reject the evidence.

But simply acknowledging the existence of a supreme being is not enough. Einstein acknowledged a cosmic force in the universe but thought God was unknowable. He thought of God as a floating cosmic battery, a sort of great electrical current that discharged one day and the universe resulted. A popular self-help organization tells its members, "You have to have a relationship with God *as you perceive Him to be.*" That is folly. How you perceive God to be apart from the revelation of Him in Scripture has nothing to do with how He is in reality.

GOD IS A PERSON

God is not just a cosmic force. Our attributes of emotion, intellect, and will did not just happen—God made us in His image. He has revealed Himself in the Bible to be a person. The Bible uses personal titles to describe Him. He is called Father. He is pictured as a shepherd. He is called a brother, a friend, a counselor. Scripture uses personal pronouns to refer to Him.

We know God is a person because He thinks, acts, feels, speaks, and communicates. All the evidence of cre-

ation, all the evidence of the Scriptures, indicates that He
is a person.

## GOD IS A SPIRIT BEING

God is a spirit. He does not exist in a body that can be
touched and seen like our bodies. And an understanding
of that, Jesus said, is essential to acceptable worship:
"God is spirit, and those who worship Him must worship
in spirit and truth" (John 4:24).

God cannot be reduced either to a physical image or a
theological abstract. He is a personal spirit, and He must
be worshiped in the fullness of the infinity of His eternal
being. Isaiah 40:18-26 explains the concept:

> To whom then will ye liken God? Or what likeness will
> you compare with Him? As for the idol, a craftsman
> casts it, a goldsmith plates it with gold, and a silver-
> smith fashions chains of silver. He who is too impover-
> ished for such an offering selects a tree that does not
> rot; he seeks out for himself a skillful craftsman to pre-
> pare an idol that will not totter. Do you not know?
> Have you not heard? Has it not been declared to you
> from the beginning? Have you not understood from the
> foundations of the earth? It is He who sits above the
> vault of the earth, and its inhabitants are like grass-
> hoppers, who stretches out the heavens like a curtain
> and spreads them out like a tent to dwell in. It is He
> who reduces rulers to nothing, who makes the judges
> of the earth meaningless. Scarcely have they been
> planted, scarcely have they been sown, scarcely has
> their stock taken root in the earth, but He merely blows
> on them and they wither, and the storm carries them
> away like stubble. "To whom then will you liken Me,
> that I should be his equal?" says the Holy One. Lift up
> your eyes on high and see who has created these stars,
> the One who leads forth their host by number, He calls
> them all by name; Because of the greatness of His
> might and the strength of His power not one of them is
> missing.

In other words, if you try to reduce God to something

other than a spirit, something that can be seen and touched, what are you going to make to represent Him? Can you draw a picture of Him? Can you carve an image like Him? Can you melt down silver and make it into a statue of Him? What are you going to make it like? To what are you going to compare it? How can you adequately represent God with an idol or an image? You can't. He is the God of the universe, and He cannot be carved out of a little piece of wood.

We must be careful not to think of God in human terms. Numbers 23:19 says, "God is not a man." When the Bible talks about the eyes of the Lord, or the arm of the Lord, and so on, it is using what we call anthropomorphisms. That comes from two Greek words, *anthropos*, meaning "man," and *morphae*, meaning "body." An anthropomorphism speaks of God in human terms to enable us to understand the concept better. The Bible uses such word pictures to accommodate our limited understanding, and we must take care not to insist on interpreting them too literally. God is not a man. The Bible talks about God's feathers covering His children. But God is not a bird, either.

First Timothy 1:17 speaks of Him as the invisible God. John 1:18 says, "No man has seen God at any time." No man will ever see God. God represented Himself to the Israelites in the Old Testament through the pillar of light and the pillar of fire and through the Shekinah glory in the Temple. At times God manifested Himself in special ways, such as in a burning bush and through visions. But those appearances did not reveal the real essence of God. God is spirit.

GOD IS ONE

Deuteronomy 6:4 was the key to God's revelation of Himself in the Old Testament: "Hear, O Israel! The Lord is our God, the Lord is one!" The truth that there is one God was fundamental to the Hebrew identity and distinctive of the Israelite nation. The Israelites, living in the midst of a polytheistic society, were saying, "There is only one God." Although they had lived among the Egyptians, whose many gods were carried to preposterous extremes, they had held to their faith in Jehovah as the one true God. God had revealed Himself to them as one God, and any Israelite who dared to worship another God was put to death.

Jesus affirmed the importance of monotheistic theology. In Mark 12, a scribe asked Him what was the greatest of the commandments. He said, "The foremost is, 'HEAR, O ISRAEL; THE LORD OUR GOD IS ONE LORD; AND YOU SHALL LOVE THE LORD YOUR GOD WITH ALL YOUR HEART, AND WITH ALL YOUR SOUL, AND WITH ALL YOUR MIND, AND WITH ALL YOUR STRENGTH'" (vv. 29-30). Without denying His own deity, and yet at the same time acknowledging that there is only one God, Jesus taught that the greatest commandment is to give total allegiance with all your heart, soul, mind, and strength to the one true God.

## THE FATHER AND THE SON ARE ONE

In John 10:30, Jesus said, "I and the Father are one." That is a claim to equality with God, and at the same time it is a reaffirmation that there is but one God.

Paul emphasized the unity and equality of the Father and the Son in his first epistle to the Corinthians. The Corinthians were living in a pagan society. Idols were everywhere in the city, and those who worshiped them would bring offerings of food. The priests of the idols' temples operated food markets, where they sold the uneaten food that had been offered to the idols. Some believers were buying that food, perhaps because they could get it for a better price than the food at conventional markets.

Other Christians were disturbed about those who were eating food that had been offered to idols. They would go over for dinner and then refuse to eat if they found out the food had come from idol offerings. It was causing serious problems in their fellowship, and Paul wrote 1 Corinthians 8 to tell them how to resolve the issue. Verse 4 sums up his teaching: "Therefore concerning the eating of things sacrificed to idols, we know that there is no such thing as an idol in the world, and that there is no God but one." An idol isn't anything. If food offered to idols is the best bargain in town, get it. Eat it. It isn't going to make a bit of difference, spiritually. An idol is nothing. And there is no other God but one.

He continues,

> For even if there are so-called gods whether in heaven or on earth, as indeed there are many gods and many Lords, yet for us there is but one God, the Father, from whom are all things, and we exist in Him; and one Lord, Jesus Christ, by whom are all things, and we exist through Him. [vv. 5-6]

How can all things be by God, the Father, and all things be by the Lord Jesus, and we exist through God and we exist through the Lord Jesus? At the surface, it might seem like a contradiction, but clearly, Paul is teaching that God the Father and the Lord Jesus Christ are one. It is another claim to the absolute deity of Jesus Christ without dividing God into parts.

### THE FATHER AND THE SPIRIT ARE ONE

The Holy Spirit also is specifically called God. To Ananias, Peter said, "Ananias, why has Satan filled your heart to lie to the Holy Spirit, and to keep back some of the price of the land?" (Acts 5:3). Then in the next verse, he spells it out: "You have not lied to men, but to God." If lying to the Holy Spirit constitutes lying to God, it necessarily follows that the Holy Spirit is in fact God.

First Corinthians 3:16 says, "Don't you know that you are a temple of God?" And as proof, it adds, "The Spirit of God lives in you." In chapter 6 the argument is carried further. Verse 19 says, "Your body is a temple of the Holy Spirit who is in you." And verse 20 adds the exhortation "Therefore glorify God in your body." That equates the Holy Spirit with God. Along with dozens of other verses, indeed the entire teaching of the New Testament, it underscores this truth: the Holy Spirit is God.

GOD IS A TRINITY

How can we reconcile the fact that Scripture teaches that the Father is God, Jesus is God, and the Holy Spirit is God, and yet there is but one God? All those truths are clearly taught in the Scriptures repeatedly.

The simplest way to perceive the Trinity is to read the Bible from the beginning to the end. The word for God in Genesis 1 is *Elohim*. It is plural. The *im* ending on a noun in Hebrew is like *s* in English. The opening words of Genesis could be translated, "In the beginning, God*s.*" The noun is plural and yet, it is clearly a singular concept. The verb that goes with it is singular.

The benediction God gave Moses for the priests to use seems to allude to the Trinity. Three times they were to invoke the blessing of the Lord. Numbers 6:24-26 records it: "The Lord bless you and keep you. The Lord make His face shine on you, and be gracious to you; the Lord lift up His countenance upon you, and give you peace." The threefold appeal to the Lord suggests the Trinity.

The seraphim Isaiah saw and described in Isaiah 6 cried to one another, "Holy, Holy, Holy" (v. 3). Again, it seems to be an allusion to the trinitarian nature of God.

The clearest Old Testament reference to the Trinity is Isaiah 48:16, a prophetic verse spoken by Jesus Christ. It puts all three members of the godhead together in one verse: "And now the Lord God has sent Me, and His Spirit."

Repeatedly the New Testament refers to the Father, Son, and Holy Spirit together in the same passage, on the same level. In Matthew 3 we are told that as Jesus was being baptized, the Holy Spirit descended as a dove, and the Father said, "This is my beloved Son, in whom I am well-pleased" (v. 17). In John 14:16-17, Jesus says, "I will ask the Father, and He will give you another Helper...that is the Spirit of truth." Jesus told His disciples to baptize "in the name of the Father and the Son and the Holy Spirit" (Matthew 28:19). In 1 Corinthians 12 the apostle Paul says, "Now there are varieties of gifts, but the same Spirit. And there are vari-

eties of ministries, and the same Lord. And there are
varieties of effects, but the same God" (vv. 4-6). The
final verse of 2 Corinthians says, "The grace of the Lord
Jesus Christ, and the love of God, and the fellowship of
the Holy Spirit, be with you all" (13:14). First Peter 1:2
says that believers are chosen "according to the fore-
knowledge of God the Father, by the sanctifying work of
the Spirit, that you may obey Jesus Christ and be sprinkled with His blood."

God is one, yet He is three. I haven't got the faintest
idea how to resolve that divine mystery, but my inability
to understand it doesn't diminish my faith in God or my
conviction that He exists as one in three Persons.

I cannot comprehend all that God has revealed about
Himself. All that I can write about God, when compared
to the totality of His attributes, is like one grain of sand
compared to every piece in the universe. If I understood
God, I would be equal to God, but He tolerates no equals.

Heretics over the centuries have tried to explain the
Trinity in several ways. Sabellius said that at times God
appears as the Holy Spirit, at other times as the Son, and
other times as the Father—just one person, with three
manifestations. But the Bible does not support that. God
is not a quick-change artist. And as we have seen, at
Jesus' baptism all three Persons of the Trinity were manifested at once. God is one and yet He is three at the very
same time.

Preachers have tried to explain the Trinity with illus-
trations, saying that God is like an egg with the yolk,
the white, and the shell; or like water, which can be
ice, liquid, or vapor; or like light, which can illumi-
nate, warm, and produce energy. But all those illustra-
tions fall short. God is not like anything. There is not a
light bulb or an egg or a chunk of ice in the world like
Him.

The Trinity is one of those truths that is just too great
for the human mind. It can only frustrate those who pursue it intellectually. God has allowed us a glimpse of it,
but we cannot hope to understand it in its fullness. We
must simply and confidently believe it.

GOD IS, AND WE CAN KNOW HIM

True worship has as its object the true God. As we saw in the first chapter, worship, no matter how beautiful or consistent or well-intentioned it is, is unacceptable if it is directed to a false God.

There is no need to erect an altar to "the unknown god," because God has made Himself knowable. He has revealed Himself to us specifically in His Word. He is a person, and we can know Him personally. He is a spirit, and we can know Him in the deepest spiritual sense. He is one, and there is no competition between Him and other gods. He is a trinity, working as one on our behalf. And He is a rewarder of those who come to Him in faith.

If our worship is to be meaningful, if it is to be acceptable, we must seek to conceive of God as He has revealed Himself to us. An intimate knowledge of the person of God is perhaps the greatest motivation to true, overflowing, whole-life worship. When we begin to know God as He is, our response has to be that of magnifying Him, giving Him glory for who He is and what He does for us.

# 5

# The Unchanging,
# Omnipotent God

In Hosea 6:6 the Lord says, "I delight in loyalty rather than sacrifice, and in the knowledge of God rather than burnt offerings." That statement elevates the knowledge of God to a position of supreme importance. It means that true worship consists not of the externals, like sacrifices, burnt offerings, and ritual, but rather is grounded in the crucial matter of knowing and loving the true God. More than He desires any external act or ritual we might think of as worship, God desires that we know Him. The knowledge of the true God, then, provides the intimacy of acceptable worship.

Proverbs 9:10 says, "The fear of the LORD is the beginning of wisdom, and the knowledge of the Holy One is understanding." No one is wise until he knows God; no one has even the slightest understanding until he has the knowledge of the Holy One. Without the knowledge of God, all worship is unacceptable worship, not any different from the grossest idolatry.

When we think of idolatry we usually think of a primitive pagan in a mud hut bowing down to a little god on the ground, or we imagine a pagan temple, very elaborate and ornate with a lot of burning incense. But idolatry goes beyond the idea of creating a false God. Fundamentally, idolatry is thinking thoughts about God that are untrue of Him, or entertaining thoughts about Him that are unworthy of Him.

In that sense, many evangelicals are guilty of idolatry. I am appalled at what some Christians assume God to be. God is appalled, too, when He says in Psalm 50:21, "You thought that I was just like you; I will reprove you, and state the case in order before your eyes." Contemporary Christianity has lowered God to its level, robbing Him of majesty and holiness. That is as idolatrous as worshiping a rock.

Yet that is precisely what many have done. They have made God into their own likeness. Their thoughts about Him come from the imaginations of their own minds, and have nothing to do with what He really is like.

A. W. Tozer wrote,

The history of mankind will probably show that no people has ever risen above its religion, and man's spiritual history will positively demonstrate that no religion has ever been greater than its idea of God. Worship is pure or base, as the worshiper entertains high or low thoughts of God.

For this reason the gravest question before the Church is always God Himself, and the most portentous fact about any man is not what he at a given time may say or do but what he in his deep heart conceives God to be like.[1]

The most basic truth in worship, then, is the worshiper's understanding of God.

But can we understand God? The Bible says we can. God promised, "And you will seek Me and find Me, when you search for Me with all your heart" (Jeremiah 29:13). Solomon wrote Proverbs 2:3:

> For if you cry for discernment,
> Lift your voice for understanding;

1. A. W. Tozer, *The Knowledge of the Holy* (New York: Harper & Row, 1961), p. 9.

If you seek her as silver,
And search for her as for hidden treasures;
Then you will discern the fear of the Lord,
And discover the knowledge of God.

The only way to know God and understand all that is revealed about God, is to make the knowledge of God the primary pursuit of your life. If you are consumed with looking for money, if you are devoted to looking for success, if you are involved with looking for anything else more than the knowledge of God, you will not deeply understand His glory.

## THE DIFFICULTY IN KNOWING GOD

Yet no one perfectly understands God. We do well to admit that God is incomprehensible; He cannot be limited by any kind of human definition. Although He has revealed much about Himself to us, everything we know about God we know in the most primitive terms.

We get into trouble when we try to make God too much like what we know. When we use human symbols to describe God, we must remember that He is the ultimate, infinite pattern and not the copy. No metaphor can fully explain God. For example, we understand God's love because we know human love. But when God's love behaves unlike our love we must not assume that God's love is faulty. That is making human love the absolute pattern and judging God's love by it.

It is often easier to think of God in negative terms. We live in a world that is so opposite God that we frequently have to grasp what God is like by saying what He is not like, because He is unlike anything we understand. For example, when we say God is holy, we mean He has no sin. We cannot conceive of the essence of absolute holiness—all we have experienced is sin. We cannot comprehend eternality or infinity, but we understand boundaries, so we say that God doesn't have any limitations.

Another difficulty in understanding God is that the attributes we know of Him are not all there are. An attribute of God is anything true of God's character. If God is infinite, there must be an infinity of truth about Him.

Some attributes of God are easier for us to comprehend than for the angels. First Peter 1 says that the angels would like to understand the truths of salvation but don't. They cannot perceive the reality of forgiveness like we can—they have never experienced it. The angels that fell were damned. The angels that did not fall did not need forgiveness. According to Ephesians 3:10, God displays Himself to angels by demonstrating His wisdom. They do understand that, perhaps better than we do.

One thing is certain: when we get to heaven, God will be much more to us than He is now. Although we may never completely comprehend the infinite richness of His attributes, He will increase our understanding and ability to experience Him. Paul wrote, "For now we see in a mirror dimly, but then face to face; now I know in part, but then I shall know fully just as I also have been fully known" (1 Corinthians 13:12).

Nevertheless, we can know for now all we need to know about God through the revelation He has given us in His Word. In the last chapter, we discovered generally who God is. In these next three chapters we want to focus on what He is like by looking more closely at some of His specific attributes.

GOD IS IMMUTABLE

First, the Bible teaches that God is not susceptible to change. He is unchangeable and unchanging. Psalm 102:25-26 says,

The heavens are the work of Thy hands.
Even they will perish, but Thou dost endure;
And all of them will wear out like a garment;
Like clothing Thou wilt change them, and they will
   be changed.
But Thou art the same,
And Thy years will not come to an end.

In Malachi 3:6 God explains the reasons He has not

totally destroyed the disobedient sons of Jacob: "For I, the Lord, do not change; therefore you, O sons of Jacob, are not consumed." James wrote, in James 1:17, "Every good thing bestowed and every perfect gift is from above, coming down from the Father of lights, with whom there is no variation, or shifting shadow."

God does not change. Change is either for the better or for the worse. Both are inconceivable with God—He couldn't get any better and wouldn't get any worse. There is nothing about Him to change.

When we say that God doesn't change, we mean that He never changes His character or His will. Numbers 23:19 says, "God is not a man, that He should lie, nor a son of man, that He should repent." He may, however, choose to react differently to man's varying responses. For example, God commanded Jonah to preach to the city of Nineveh that they would be destroyed. But at the preaching of Jonah, the whole city repented. The Bible says, "God relented concerning the calamity which He had declared He would bring upon them. And He did not do it." Instead of destroying them He blessed them. Did God change? No, it was Nineveh that changed, and God responded to their repentance with a blessing, which is consistent with His nature.

Genesis 6:6 says that when God looked at the debauchery of mankind in the pre-Flood civilization, He "was sorry that He had made man on the earth." God had made man for blessing, and man had turned God's blessing into a curse. God's will and His character were unchanged. He would reward good and punish evil. But man had changed, and God was sorry for what man would suffer in judgment. He has no joy when judgment falls (2 Peter 3:9).

When the Bible says God was sorry, it doesn't mean that He thought He had made a mistake. The King James Version uses the word *repented*. That doesn't mean He changed His mind. The Bible simply expresses in terms we can understand a divine attitude of grief over sin. It means God responded to man's iniquity with sorrow and altered His treatment of mankind in accordance with

how they were behaving. His will never changed. He
never varied from His course (cf. Jeremiah 13:17).

God's immutability sets Him apart from everything,
because everything else changes. The whole universe is
changing. Galaxies die and begin. Even the sun is slowly
burning out. Our world is constantly changing. The sea-
sons change. We grow old and die, and from the beginning to the end, all we know is change.

Not God. He is "the same yesterday and today, yes and
forever" (Hebrews 13:8).

## THE BLESSING OF GOD'S IMMUTABILITY

That God does not change is a great source of comfort
to believers. It means that His love is forever. His forgiveness is forever. His salvation is forever. His promises are
forever.

In Romans 11:29, Paul writes, "The gifts and the calling of God are irrevocable." God doesn't change His
promise. "If we are faithless, He remains faithful; for He
cannot deny Himself" (2 Timothy 2:13). If our faith runs
low He doesn't change toward us. The security of salvation, then, is based on God's unchanging character.

For the Christian, the knowledge that God is immutable is reassuring and exciting. We belong to Him, and
He has promised to supply all our needs. We are secure in
our relationship with Him. His love for us will never
diminish; He will indeed finish the work He began in us
(cf. Philippians 1:6).

For an unbeliever, however, the knowledge that God
does not change can be terrifying. God has said that the
soul that sins will die. He will not alter His decree. His
Word says that the wages of sin is death, and that will be
just as true at the final judgment as it was when it was
written. Although He may feel grief, God will not soften
His position on sin. The Bible says in Psalm 119:89,
"Forever, O Lord, thy word is settled in heaven."

## GOD IS OMNIPOTENT

Fifty-six times in the Bible the word *almighty* is used.
Always it is used of God; never of anyone else. God is all

powerful, or omnipotent. Again we are forced to use a negative to explain the concept—there is nothing He can't do. That is a staggering idea. He has no bounds to His energy.

God can do one thing as easily as He can do another. It is no more difficult for God to create a universe than it is for Him to make a butterfly, and He does everything without losing any of His strength. Isaiah 40:28 says, "The Everlasting God, the Lord, the Creator of the ends of the earth does not become weary or tired." God never needs to be replenished. Where would He go for more strength? There is no power outside of God.

Built into absolute power is the authority to use it. God not only has the power but He also has the authority to do anything He wants to do. While God can do anything He wants to do, however, His will is totally consistent with His nature. That's why, for example, He cannot lie and will not tolerate sin. It is also why He shows grace and mercy. Psalm 115:3 says, "Our God is in the heavens; He does whatever He pleases." Have you ever asked the question "Why did God do this?" He did it because He wanted to. If that doesn't seem like a sufficient answer to you, it's because you don't understand God. You are trying to make Him like men.

In Romans 9 Paul deals with the issue of God's doing whatever He wants, and he suggests that some will raise the question "Why does He still find fault? For who resists His will?" (v. 19). In other words, If God is always doing what He wants, how can He fault men? The answer he then gives is not likely to satisfy those who do not understand God's absolute power: "Who are you, O man, who answers back to God? The thing molded will not say to the molder, 'Why did you make me like this,' will it?" (v. 20). In other words, we have no right to question God. The ultimate power of design is the potter's right.

There are four areas in which God's power can be seen most clearly. One is *His ability to create something from nothing*. Psalm 33:6 says, "By the word of the Lord the heavens were made, and by the breath of His mouth all their host." Verse 9 adds, "He spoke, and it was done; He commanded, and it stood fast." Romans 4:17 says He "calls into being that which does not exist." He created everything without any help. Isaiah 44:24 says, "I, the Lord, am the maker of all things, stretching out the heavens by Myself, and spreading out the earth all alone." The universe came into existence the moment God had the thought: *world*. Instantly, there it was.

Think about the power in the created universe. We can split an atom and with the resulting explosion destroy a major city. But even if men could set off a chain reaction that would engulf the entire universe, it would not approach the infinite power of God, because God is greater than anything He ever made. He is the one who put all that potential power into every tiny atom.

A second area in which God's power can be seen is in *His ability to sustain His creation*. Hebrews 1:3 says He "upholds all things by the word of His power." God rested on the seventh day of creation, but not because He was tired. In fact, He didn't really rest, in the sense that we think of rest. He just ceased His creative activity. If God had stopped functioning on the seventh day, everything He made on the first six would have fallen apart.

When God rested on the seventh day, He was also establishing a physical and spiritual pattern for us, as well as a symbol of rest to be ultimately fulfilled in the plan of eternal redemption in Christ Jesus. We need physical rest and time for worship and spiritual replenishing. But God doesn't. He continues to preserve His creation.

Further, God's power is clearly visible in *His ability to redeem the lost*. In fact, His power is more wondrous in redemption than in creation, because in creation there was no opposition, no devil to be subdued, no thundering law to be silenced, no death to be conquered, no sin to be pardoned, no hell to be shut, no death on the cross to be suffered.

What makes redemption truly startling is that God called to Himself a selection of nobodies and made them confound the mighty. First Corinthians 1:26-28 says,

For consider your calling, brethren, that there were not many wise according to the flesh, not many mighty, not many noble; but God has chosen the foolish things of the world to confound the wise, and God has chosen the weak things of the world to shame the things which are strong, and the base things of the world and the despised, God has chosen, the things that are not, that He might nullify the things that are.

The first few chapters of Acts show how the apostles turned the world upside down. It was a clear demonstration of God's power in redemption.

Finally, God's limitless power is visible in *His ability to raise the dead*. Someday at the end of the age, God is going to raise from the dead every human being that ever lived, righteous and unrighteous. Jesus said, "An hour is coming, in which all who are in the tombs shall hear His voice, and shall come forth; those who did the good deeds to a resurrection of life, those who committed the evil deeds to a resurrection of judgment" (John 5:28-29). That speaks of incomprehensible resurrection power.

Who can comprehend the ability to bring someone back from the dead? Yet Jesus did it repeatedly during His earthly ministry and capped it all with His own resurrection, as the firstfruits of all who have died to be raised to glory.

THE MEANING OF GOD'S OMNIPOTENCE

That God is omnipotent is another practical truth, fundamental to true worship. Second Kings 17:36 says, "But the Lord, who brought you up from the land of Egypt with great power and with an outstretched arm, Him you shall fear, and to Him you shall bow yourselves down." The King James Version says, "Him shall ye worship."

An understanding of God's omnipotence is a strong motivation to worship, because for the Christian, God's power is a basis of daily confidence in Him. When I feel inadequate and unable to do anything, I am reminded of Philippians 4:13, which says, "I can do all things through Him who strengthens me." Ephesians 3:20 says that God is "able to do exceeding abundantly beyond all that we ask or think, according to the power that works within us." God's power sustains us in our daily lives.

That is a great source of encouragement. No problem we face is too hard for Him to handle. Psalm 121:1-2 gives us this perspective: "I will lift up my eyes to the mountains; from whence shall my help come? My help comes from the Lord, who made heaven and earth." God made heaven and earth. None of our problems are a match for His great power.

Ephesians 6:10 says, "Be strong in the Lord, and in the strength of His might." We don't need to fight our battles in our own energy; His omnipotent power is available to us. When the adversary comes, don't fight. Go tell the Commander. He fights for us, and the secret to our victory is relying on His power. John wrote, "Greater is He who is in you than he who is in the world" (1 John 4:4).

There is no need to fear falling away or losing our salvation. Paul wrote to Timothy, "I am not ashamed; for I know whom I have believed and I am convinced that He is able to guard what I have entrusted to Him until that day" (2 Timothy 1:12).

Romans 8:33-35 asks, "Who will bring a charge against God's elect? . . . Who shall separate us from the love of Christ? Shall tribulation, or distress, or persecution, or famine, or nakedness, or peril, or sword?" No. God is all-powerful. Paul goes on, "I am convinced that neither death, nor life, nor angels, nor principalities, nor things present, nor things to come, nor powers, nor height, nor depth, nor any other created thing, shall be able to separate us from the love of God, which is in Christ Jesus our Lord" (vv. 38-39).

But for unbelievers, the implication of God's omnipotence is quite different. An unbeliever is in opposition to God, and for him, God's power is a threat. It means that his judgment is sure, and "It is a terrifying thing to fall into the hands of the living God" (Hebrews 10:31).

## WORSHIPING THE UNCHANGING, OMNIPOTENT GOD

We worship an unchanging, all-powerful God. If that makes Him seem far beyond your ability to comprehend, that is good. If you think of God as someone simple enough for the human mind to understand, your god is not the true God.

What is your concept of God? Do you see Him as a timeless, infinite, all-powerful, unchanging, glorious being? Or do you, like many, tend to minimize God's greatness, preferring to think of Him as one who may be manipulated or fooled by human hypocrisy, or one who may be mandated to do what we want? Such a view of God is utterly pagan.

A vision of the steadfastness of our immutable God brings a sense of security and stability to our unsettled lives. And the understanding that His power is unlimited and undiminishing strengthens and encourages even the weakest believer. The natural response to that is praise and adoration that overflows in a life that worships.

# 6

# The God Who Is Everywhere—and Knows Everything

In 1 Chronicles 28:9, David told his son, "As for you, my son Solomon, know the God of your father, and serve Him with a whole heart and a willing mind." That is the finest advice. Know God; and when you know Him, serve Him willingly with a perfect heart. David continues, "For the LORD searches all hearts, and understands every intent of the thoughts. If you seek Him, He will let you find Him; but if you forsake Him, He will reject you forever." We could wish every father gave that message to his son.

As that verse implies, the consequences of not knowing God are grim. In 2 Thessalonians 1:7-8 Paul wrote, "The Lord Jesus will be revealed from heaven with His mighty angels in flaming fire, dealing out retribution to those who do not know God."

To know God, you see, is to have eternal life. The one who knows God intimately partakes of His very nature and life. In John 17:3, our Lord prayed, "And this is eternal life, that they may know Thee, the only true God."

Wisdom is wrapped up in the idea of knowing God. Solomon wrote,

Make your ear attentive to wisdom, incline your heart
to understanding; for if you cry for discernment, lift
your voice for understanding; if you seek her as silver,
and search for her as hidden treasures; then you will
discern the fear of the Lord, and discover the
knowledge of God. [Proverbs 2:2-5]

The knowledge of God is the product of wisdom. A man is
wise to the degree he understands the true God.

God wants us to know Him. He is not hiding. God is not
some sort of cosmic hide-and-seek player stashed in a
bush, saying, "You're getting warmer." God is not trying
to cover Himself up. He has disclosed Himself, and He
wants us to know Him.

In the previous chapter, we scratched the surface of
just two attributes of God—His immutability and His
omnipotence. In this chapter we will examine two more.

## GOD IS OMNIPRESENT

People have always tried to confine God. Many Old
Testament Jews felt that God actually dwelt in the Temple. They did not understand that it was only the symbol
of His presence and He did not dwell there in His fullness.
People in our society tend to think of God as off somewhere in a celestial palace. But God cannot be limited to
any place. God is everywhere at all times, or
omnipresent.

" 'Am I a God who is near,' declares the Lord, 'and not
a God far off? Can a man hide himself in hiding places so
I do not see him?' declares the Lord. 'Do I not fill the
heavens and the earth?' declares the Lord" (Jeremiah
23:23). In other words, God is not an idol confined to a
location. He cannot be contained in a building. We don't
go somewhere to worship because God is there. That is
an utterly heathen notion.

The Assyrians thought the God of the Israelites lived in
the hill and their gods lived in the valleys. Some of the
pagans thought their gods lived in groves especially prepared for them.

According to 1 Samuel 5, when the Philistines stole the

Ark of the Covenant, they thought it was the representation of the God of the Israelites. They took the Ark and put it in the temple of their god, Dagon. They figured that's where their gods lived, so why not put the Israelite God there?

The next morning, the statue of Dagon was dumped over on its face. So they put it back up. The next day it was dumped over again, and this time its hands and head were cut off. God had performed supernatural surgery on that idol. First Samuel 5:5 says, "Therefore neither the priests of Dagon nor all who enter Dagon's house tread on the threshold of Dagon in Ashdod to this day." Nobody ever went into the temple of Dagon at Ashdod again. Who wants to worship a god who is victimized by a more powerful God?

They associated their god with that place. But the true God doesn't dwell in temples made with hands. He cannot be confined to a single location or building or object. He is everywhere and everywhere available to a true worshiper.

Occasionally the language of Scripture may seem to imply that God moved from place to place, such as in Genesis 11:5, which says, "And the Lord came down to see the city and the tower which the sons of men had built." That verse is simply putting a difficult truth in language we can understand. It means, from a human perspective, that He gave the city and the tower His immediate attention. God didn't have to travel to get there. Just because God acted uniquely in one place, at one time, for one special reason, did not mean He wasn't everywhere else at the same time.

WHERE DOES GOD DWELL?

What does the Bible mean when it speaks of God's dwelling place? For example, the New Testament teaches that He indwells believers. Is God only in the hearts of believers? Is He not also in the hearts of wicked men?

When the Bible says that believers are the temples of God (1 Corinthians 3:16), it is speaking of a special relationship God has with those who are redeemed. It speaks of a relational, spiritual presence. God in His essence is present with everyone, but He has a unique indwelling relationship with believers.

In the Old Testament, God is said to have dwelt between the wings of the cherubim on the Ark of the Covenant. That simply means that the Holy of Holies was a special place where God established the throne of His majesty symbolically.

Today the church serves that purpose. Believers are temples, the symbols of God's majestic presence. In the kingdom, the throne of God will be represented by a throne in Jerusalem where Christ reigns. In heaven it is represented by the throne pictured in Revelation 4 and 5. Those are all simply symbols, and the symbol of God's presence is never the prison of His essence. God is everywhere.

God is even in places we associate with evil. He is in the heart of a sinner by inspection and conviction. He is in hell by His acts of judgement, for it is He who is able to destroy both soul and body in hell. That does not mean He is defiled by the impurity around Him. His essence is everywhere, but it never mingles with any impurity. In a sense, God is like the sun's rays. A sunbeam may fall on a rotting corpse in a field, but that corpse never lays any of its corruption on the sunbeam.

God is purely the essence of who He is, unmixed with anything. Nothing defiles Him. Jesus came into the world, walked through the world, saw sin, and fellowshiped with sinners, yet there was no sin in Him. God can touch anything and be undefiled by it.

It is a staggering thought. God is everywhere, and He is unmixed with anything. Nothing corrupts Him. Nothing touches Him to change His character in any way at all. What kind of practical application does that doctrine have?

THE BELIEVER'S RESPONSE TO GOD'S PRESENCE

First, it means assurance. Whatever adverse circumstances or emotions we experience, whether we realize He is there or not, God is there. We may doubt His presence, we may feel as if He were far away, but He is as near as He always has been. "He Himself has said, 'I will never desert you, nor will I ever forsake you' " (Hebrews 13:5). Philippians 4:5-6 includes this phrase: "The Lord is near. Be anxious for nothing." Although that verse is often understood to be talking about the Second Coming, it actually refers to Christ's perpetual presence. He's there all the time. Realize it. It is one of His attributes, an integral part of His character.

Can a Christian be separated from God? No! No one in the universe can be separated from God essentially, and a believer cannot be separated from Him relationally, either. He is always there. In 2 Timothy 2:13, we are told that even if our faith begins to falter, He abides faithfully. Unbroken fellowship is the symbol of the believer. God is with us now as much as He will be with us in eternity. He dwells within us. That is a great source of assurance.

God's presence also means support for the believer. When God called Moses, Moses said in Exodus 4:10, "Please, Lord, I have never been eloquent, neither recently nor in time past . . . for I am slow of speech and slow of tongue." God's answer was, "I, even I, will be with your mouth."

To say that God is present doesn't mean He is just standing there watching. It means that He is there in support of our work for Him. When Christ gave the disciples the mandate we know as the Great Commission, He punctuated it with this promise: "And lo, I am with you always, even unto the end of the age" (Matthew 28:20). It was His assurance that work done for Him would be blessed by His presence and powerful aid.

God's continuing presence is also a shield against overwhelming temptation. Any time Satan wants to get to a believer, he has to go through God. First Corinthians 10:13 says, "No temptation has overtaken you but such as is common to man; and God is faithful, who will not allow you to be tempted beyond what you are able, but with the temptation will provide a way of escape also, that you may be able to endure it." God is present personally and individually with every believer to defend him against temptation he couldn't handle.

That God is present everywhere ought to motivate us to obey Him more carefully. When we sin, whether it is a sin of thought or a sin of words or a sin of actions, it is done in the presence of God. It is as if we ascended the clouds, came into the throne room of God, walked up to the foot of the throne of God and performed the sin right there. That is a sobering thought.

Proverbs 3:6 implies just that when it says, "In all your ways acknowledge Him." Living the Christian life means ordering my life with the understanding that everything I do is done in the presence of God. That should revolutionize our "private" lives.

### THE OTHER SIDE OF THE COIN

To believers then, the doctrine of omnipresence is extremely important, but what does it mean to an unbeliever? An evil man has no hiding place. There is no escape, no way out, no place for him to retreat. Amos 9:2-4 gives insight into the plight of the unbeliever who tries to hide from God:

> Though they dig into Sheol,
> From there shall My hand take them;
> And though they ascend to Heaven,
> From there will I bring them down.
> And though they hide on the summit of Carmel,
> I will search them out and take them from there;
> And though they conceal themselves from My sight
>     on the floor of the sea,
> From there will I command the serpent and it will
>     bite them.
> And though they go into captivity before their
>     enemies,
> From there I will command the sword that it slay
>     them,
> And I will set My eyes against them for evil and not for
>     good.

There is no place to hide. The ungodly man must realize that no matter how he tries, no matter how he runs, he cannot escape God. He may decide he doesn't want to go to church, he doesn't want to read the Bible, he wants to avoid any religious discussion, he wants to put God out of his mind—but God is there.

Job 26:5-6 says, "The departed spirits tremble under the waters and their inhabitants. Naked is Sheol before Him and Abaddon has no covering." God unmasks everything by His presence. Job 34:21 says, "For His eyes are upon the ways of a man, and He sees all his steps. There is no darkness or deep shadow where the workers of iniquity may hide themselves."

In Psalm 139, David says,

> Where can I go from Thy Spirit?
> Or where can I flee from Thy presence?
> If I ascend to heaven, Thou art there;
> If I make my bed in Sheol, behold, Thou art there.
> If I take the wings of the dawn,
> If I dwell in the remotest part of the sea,
> Even there Thy hand will lead me,
> And Thy right hand will lay hold of me.
> If I say, "surely the darkness will overwhelm me,
> And the light around me will be night,"
> Even the darkness is not dark to Thee,
> And the night is as bright as day.
> Darkness and light are alike to Thee.
>
> vv. 7-12

The thief steals when he thinks no one sees. The adulterer commits adultery when he thinks no one will know. The liar lies because he thinks no one finds out. But God knows. Just because God is invisible doesn't mean He isn't there. God never slumbers and never sleeps. Hebrews 4:13 makes a poignant statement: "And there is no creature hidden from His sight, but all things are open and laid bare to the eyes of Him with whom we have to do."

GOD IS OMNISCIENT

Closely related to God's omnipresence is the attribute

of omniscience. Psalm 147:5 says of God, "His understanding is infinite." He knows not only the knowable,
but the unknowable as well. First Samuel 2:3 says, "For
the LORD is a God of knowledge." The Hebrew word for
*knowledge* in that verse is plural, emphasizing the
extent of God's knowledge.

In Romans 16:27 Paul called Him "the only wise God."
Not only does God know everything, but He also is the
only one who does. The angels' knowledge is extensive,
but they do not know everything God knows. Man's
knowledge is increasing, but compared to God's knowledge, it is foolishness.

WHERE DOES GOD GET HIS INFORMATION?

God does not obtain His knowledge. Because He knows
everything, He doesn't need to learn. Who would teach
Him? Isaiah 40:13 asks, "Who has directed the Spirit of
the Lord, or as His counselor has informed Him?" The
answer, of course, is no one. In Romans 11:34, Paul says,
"Who has known the mind of the Lord, or who became
His counselor?" Who taught God? No one. God knows
everything, and He always has.

Our prayer requests are not meant to give God information He needs. He knows our needs before we pray. We
pray to unburden our hearts and to show we care, and
because He chooses to work through our prayers.

No knowledge is out of reach from God. There isn't a
secret thought or a secret word or a secret deed hidden
from God. He even knows the number of hairs on your
head. Why would God bother to count our hair? He
doesn't count it; He knows it. God isn't keeping a record
book on hair just to prove a point. Anything that is, He
knows. He doesn't have to learn it or find it out.

God can see beyond the exterior. In Revelation 2:23 He
says, "I am He who searches the hearts and minds." We
cannot keep secrets from God; He sees our hearts and our
minds just as well as He sees our outside. Psalm 139:4
says, "Even before there is a word on my tongue, behold,
O LORD, Thou dost know it all." God hears our whispers
as if they were broadcasts, and our minds could not con-

ceive the subtlest thought outside the knowledge of God. God says in Isaiah 66:18, "I know their . . . thoughts."

Several places in the gospels tell us that Jesus could see the hearts of men. John 2:25 says, "He knew what was in man." And Luke 6:8 says, "He knew what they were thinking." Nicodemus came to Jesus with one question with his mouth and another in his mind (John 3). Jesus answered the one in his mind although Nicodemus never asked it with his lips.

## GOD'S INFINITE WISDOM

God's omniscience is inseparable from His perfect wisdom. Wisdom is omniscience acting with a holy will. If He knows the end from the beginning, He knows every step between. And He is able to make all things work together ultimately to result in good, even if circumstances appear otherwise to us (Romans 8:28).

Consider His creation. Everything from the vastness of the universe to the detail of the microscopic world evidences staggering wisdom. The component parts of the universe extend beyond calculation, and yet everything functions in harmony with every other thing to bring about exactly what God intends. God's creation is a monument to His wisdom. Psalm 104:24 says, "O Lord, how many are Thy works! In wisdom Thou hast made them all."

## GOD KNOWS EVERYTHING—SO WHAT?

What are the practical lessons of God's omniscience? How does it affect believers? For one thing, it is a great comfort to know that God knows everything. We do not seem very significant in the universe. Have you ever wondered if God knows you are here? He does.

In Malachi's time, God was breathing down judgment on the people, and Malachi was prophesying more judgment. A group of righteous people began to wonder if they would be indiscriminately swept up in the destruction. Malachi 3:16-17 says,

Then those who feared the Lord spoke to one another.

And the Lord gave attention and heard it, and a book
of remembrance was written before Him for those who
fear the Lord and who esteem His name. "And they will
be Mine," says the Lord of hosts, "on the day that I prepare My own possession, and I will spare them as a
man spares his own son who serves him."

God has a book with the names of His people, and He
doesn't forget who belongs in it. According to Revelation
13:8, the names of believers have been recorded in God's
book from the foundation of the world as well. He knew
before time. It is a solid, comforting confidence for the
believer to know that absolutely no one is outside the
knowledge of God. He knows us, and He knows that we
belong to Him.

God knows every trial we ever go through and all our
needs. In Matthew 6:25-33, He says,

Do not be anxious for your life, as to what you shall
eat, or what you shall drink; nor for your body, as to
what you shall put on. Is not life more than food, and
the body more than clothing? Look at the birds of the
air, that they do not sow, neither do they reap, nor
gather into barns; and yet your heavenly Father feeds
them. Are you not worth much more than they? And
which of you by being anxious can add a single cubit
to his life's span? And why are you anxious about
clothing? Observe how the lilies of the field grow; they
do not toil nor do they spin, yet I say to you that even
Solomon in all his glory did not clothe himself like one
of these. But if God so arrays the grass of the field,
which is alive today and tomorrow is thrown into the
furnace, will He not much more do so for you, O men of
little faith? Do not be anxious then, saying, "What
shall we eat?" or "What shall we drink?" or "With
what shall we clothe ourselves?" For all these things
the Gentiles eagerly seek; for your heavenly Father
knows that you need all these things. But seek first His
kingdom and His righteousness; and all these things
shall be added to you.

My Father knows my needs and He takes care of them all.

## GOD KNOWS US, AND LOVES US ANYWAY

I used to think that the doctrine of omniscience was anything but reassuring. When I was young, my parents often said, "We may not know what you do, but God does. He sees everything." I thought of that as a threat, something that only made me fearful of doing anything wrong.

To be sure, God's omniscience *is* an effective deterrent to sin. God is one teacher who never leaves the room. Second Corinthians 5:10 tells us that someday we will be called to account for all the things that we've done in the body. And 1 Corinthians 4:5 says that the Lord will "bring to light the things hidden in darkness and disclose the motives of men's hearts." That is a powerful motivation to live righteously.

My parents were right; God knows everything we do. And yet His correction is always with love. Peter denied the Lord three times at His crucifixion. In John 21, the Lord confronted Peter and asked, "Do you love Me?" (v. 16). Peter assured the Lord that he loved Him. The Lord asked again—a total of three times. Finally Peter said, "Lord, You know all things; You know that I love You." Peter appealed to Jesus' omniscience rather than his own visible behavior to verify his love.

First John 3:19-20 says, "We...shall assure our heart before Him, in whatever our heart condemns us; for God is greater than our heart, and knows all things." God's omniscience does more for us than merely act as a watchdog; it is a source of our confidence and assurance, for by it He sees beyond our disobedience and failure, to a heart of love for Him.

## GOD'S OMNISCIENCE AND THE UNBELIEVER

To the unbeliever, though, the doctrine of omniscience is not such a comfort. It unmasks him and reveals the stupidity of hypocrisy. God isn't like man, who looks on the outward appearance. God looks on the heart. The notion that a man can play a game with God and get by is devastated by the truth that God knows everything. He isn't fooled.

In fact, God's omniscience stands in stark contrast to the folly of human wisdom and human hypocrisy. First Corinthians 3:18-20 says,

Let no man deceive himself. If any man among you thinks that he is wise in this age, let him become foolish that he may become wise. For the wisdom of this world is foolishness before God. For it is written, "He is the one who catches the wise in their own craftiness"; and again, "The Lord knows the reasonings of the wise, that they are useless."

God's omniscience also says to the unbeliever that there is a promise of accurate judgment. Romans 2:2 says, "The judgment of God is according to truth" (KJV). We can be certain that the final judgment will be just. God will judge on the basis of truth, because He has absolute knowledge of it. In Jeremiah 16:17 the prophet said, "They are not hidden from My face, nor is their iniquity concealed from My eyes." There is no hiding from God's judgment.

## THE CRUCIAL ISSUE

So God's attributes have a vastly different effect on believers and unbelievers. To those who trust Him, God's attributes are uplifting, encouraging, strengthening; sources of great comfort, confidence, and assurance. But to those who rebel and refuse to trust Him, God's attributes become threats, causes for fear, harbingers of eternal doom.

The character of God is established. The issue is how one responds. A man who smashes himself against God continually, trying to live the way he wants to live no matter what God is like, is a fool.

God is immutable, omnipotent, omnipresent, and omniscient. Our response to that ought to be humble, honest worship. It is easy to be proud if we focus on ourselves. But as soon as we start understanding what God is like we realize our lowliness, and our response is a desire to give God glory.

# 7

# Holy, Holy, Holy

Knowing that God is immutable, omnipotent, omnipresent, and omniscient is significant, but those attributes give limited insight into what God expects of us.
What beyond His unchanging, all-powerful, infinitely
knowing presence compels us to worship?

It is basically this: God is holy. Of all the attributes of
God, holiness is the one that most uniquely describes
Him and in reality is a summarization of all His other
attributes. The word *holiness* refers to His separateness,
His otherness, the fact that He is unlike any other being.
It indicates His complete and infinite perfection. Holiness
is the attribute of God that binds all the others together.
Properly understood, it will revolutionize the quality of
our worship.

When they exalted God, the angels didn't say, "Eternal, Eternal, Eternal,"; they didn't say, "Faithful, Faithful, Faithful,"; "Wise, Wise, Wise"; or "Mighty, Mighty,
Mighty." They said, "Holy, Holy, Holy, is the Lord God,
the Almighty" (Revelation 4:8). His holiness is the crown
of all that He is.

Exodus 15:11 asks, "Who is like Thee among the gods,
O Lord? Who is like Thee, majestic in holiness, awesome

in praises, working wonders?" The answer, of course, is that no being is equal to God in holiness. In fact, holiness is so uniquely and exclusively an attribute of God that Psalm 111:9 says, "Holy and awesome is His name."

## THE STANDARD OF ABSOLUTE HOLINESS

God doesn't conform to a holy standard; He is the standard. He never does anything wrong, He never errs, He never makes a misjudgment, He never causes something to happen that isn't right. There are no degrees to His holiness. He is holy, flawless, without error, without sin, fully righteous, utterly, absolutely, infinitely holy.

To be in God's presence, one must be holy. That was demonstrated when the angels sinned. God immediately cast them out and prepared a place for them separated from His presence. When men choose not to come to God, when they choose to reject Jesus Christ, their ultimate end is to be sent to the place prepared for the devil and his angels, out of the presence of God.

Miraculously, salvation imputes God's own holiness to the believer in Jesus Christ (see Philippians 3:8-9). Peter articulated that truth when he wrote: "It is written, 'You shall be holy, For I am holy' " (1 Peter 1:16).

God's holiness is best seen in His hatred of sin. God cannot tolerate sin; He is totally removed from it. Amos 5:21-23 records God's strong words to those attempting to worship Him while polluted with sin:

> I hate, I reject your festivals, nor do I delight in your solemn assemblies. Even though you offer up to Me burnt offerings and your grain offerings, I will not accept them; And I will not even look at the peace offerings of your fatlings. Take away from Me the noise of your songs; I will not even listen to the sound of your harps.

That does not mean that God hates sacrifices and offerings and festivals and music. God desires all those things, because He instituted them. But when those instruments of worship are tainted with sin, God hates them.

God doesn't want you to sin, even if it would make your testimony more exciting, or display His grace. He never wills sin. He will not keep you from sinning if you choose to, but God never tempts anyone to sin, and He cannot be tempted to sin (James 1:13). Sin is the object of His displeasure. God loves holiness. Psalm 11:7 says, "For the Lord is righteous; He loves righteousness."

## THE PROOF OF GOD'S HOLINESS

God's holiness is visible in many ways. It is seen *in the creation of man*, to begin with. In Ecclesiastes 7:29, we read, "Behold, I have found only this, that God made men upright, but they have sought out many devices." In other words, when God made man, He made him to reflect His holiness. Sin was man's rebellion against that purpose.

Residual marks of God's holiness are still evident in man despite man's sin. Man has an innate sense of right and wrong. Although it is imperfect, that inborn understanding of good and evil manifests itself through man's conscience, his code of ethics, and his sense of justice. Romans 1:15 describes the accountability of the Gentiles to God: "They show the work of the law written in their hearts, their conscience bearing witness, and their thoughts alternately accusing them or else defending them." Even the vilest, most rebellious man has at least a crude framework of righteousness inherent in his consciousness.

Second, God's holiness is seen *in the moral law*. One of the primary reasons God instituted the law under Moses was to demonstrate His holiness. When God laid down a legal standard of morality, He proved Himself to be a righteous, moral, holy being. In Romans 7:12 Paul says, "The law is holy, and the commandment is holy and righteous and good." The moral aspects of the Mosaic law are all reaffirmed in the teachings of the New Testament.

God's holiness is evident *in His sacrificial law*. although we might not normally think of it that way. When we see God commanding that animals be slain as sacrifices and their blood sprinkled all over, we see in a graphic way that death is the result of sin. Every time the Jews made a sacrifice, they illustrated the deadliness of sin, and that stated by contrast the holiness of God.

In a related sense, God's holiness is also seen *in judgment on sin.* When the Bible speaks, for example, as it does in 2 Thessalonians 1:7, of Jesus' coming in flaming fire and taking vengeance on those who do not know God and do not obey the gospel; and when it describes, as it does in Jude 15, the condemnation of the ungodly, we see how God hates sin. His judgment on sin is a reflection of His holiness; He must punish sin because He is holy.

The supreme demonstration of the holiness of God is seen *in the cross.* That is where God bore man's sin in the person of Christ and gave the greatest illustration of His holiness—His hatred of sin and power over it. God is so holy that He had to turn from His own Son because Christ bore man's sin. He paid the ultimate price necessary to satisfy His holiness—the death of His Son.

Hebrews 9:26 makes an amazing and mysterious statement: "He has been manifested to put away sin by the sacrifice of Himself." God in Christ paid the supreme price of dying Himself, bearing man's sin, because the price had to be paid even if it cost Him His own life. That's holiness.

WORSHIP THE LORD IN THE BEAUTY OF HOLINESS

A worshiping life must affirm the utter holiness of God; in fact, an acknowledgment and understanding of God's holiness is essential to true worship. In the words of Psalm 96:2-6, we are to:

Sing to the Lord, bless His name;
Proclaim good tidings of His salvation from day to
    day.
Tell of His glory among the nations,
His wonderful deeds among all the peoples.
For great is the Lord and greatly to be praised;
He is to be feared above all gods.
For all the gods of the peoples are idols,

But the Lord made the heavens.
Splendor and majesty are before Him,
Strength and beauty are in His sanctuary.

That describes acts of worship. Verse 9 makes the key statement: "Worship the Lord in holy attire; tremble before Him, all the earth." *Holy attire* means the spiritual clothing of holiness. *Tremble before Him* implies fear. In fact, the King James Version translates that verse, "O worship the Lord in the beauty of holiness: fear before him, all the earth."

Here we are introduced to the frequent biblical connection of the idea of God's holiness with fear on the part of the worshiper. It is a fear that grows out of an overwhelming sense of unworthiness in the presence of pure holiness. For example, in Genesis 18 Abraham confessed in the presence of God that he was dust and ashes. Similarly, Job said after his pilgrimage, "I have heard of Thee by the hearing of the ear; but now my eye sees Thee; Therefore I retract, and I repent in dust and ashes" (Job 42:5-6). Ezra 9 records Ezra's sense of shame as he came before the Lord to worship. Habakkuk saw God revealed in the midst of his trial and circumstance, and his knees began to smash together.

ISAIAH'S ENCOUNTER WITH GOD

Isaiah 6 describes Isaiah's experience with God's holiness. Uzziah had been king in Judah for 52 years. Although he was superficially effective and had secured the country from its enemies, built a very formidable army, tightened up its defenses, created economic productivity, and brought great external security; inwardly the nation was corrupt, defiled, wretched, and superficially worshiping God.

As a result, in chapter 5, Isaiah pronounced half a dozen curses on Judah. The people had the illusion that things were going along well because they had a good leader. But in 740 B.C. their leader died of leprosy when God struck him down because of his pride.

When Uzziah died, the nation's sense of security was

gone, and Isaiah sensed a tremendous need to enter into
the presence of God. In Isaiah 6:1 Isaiah describes how
he saw the Lord sitting on a throne, high and lifted up.
And there he heard the seraphim cry back and forth to
one another in antiphonal response, "Holy, Holy, Holy, is
the Lord of Hosts, the whole earth is full of His glory" (v.
3). His holiness fills all.

As Isaiah in worship perceived the holiness of God,
the posts of the place began to move at the voice of
those angels who cried back and forth, and the house
was filled with smoke. He tells us his response in verse
5: "Then I said, 'Woe is me, for I am ruined! Because I
am a man of unclean lips, and I live among a people of
unclean lips; for my eyes have seen the King, the Lord
of hosts.' "

One of the seraphim flew and touched Isaiah's mouth
with a live, hot coal as a symbol of cleansing. When he
was thus purged and made clean; the Lord was ready to
use him, and he was available (v. 8).

Some might think that Isaiah did not have a very good
self-image. He was not thinking positively; he was not
affirming his strengths. Surely, Isaiah knew that he had
the best mouth in the land! He was a prophet of God! He
was the best man in the nation. And yet he cursed himself. Why?

The answer is very clear. We find it in the words "Mine
eyes have seen the King, the Lord of Hosts" (v. 5). Isaiah
had seen a vision of God in His holiness, and he was
absolutely shattered to the very core of his being by a
sense of his own sinfulness. His heart longed for purging.

## WHATEVER HAPPENED TO THE FEAR OF GOD?

When we see God as holy, our instant and only reaction is to see ourselves as unholy. Between God's holiness and man's unholiness is a gulf. And until a man
understands the holiness of God he can never know the
depth of his own sin. We ought to be shaken to our roots
when we see ourselves in comparison to Him. If we are
not deeply pained about our sin, we do not understand
God's holiness.

Without such a vision of God's holiness, true worship is not possible. Worship is not giddy. It does not rush into God's presence unprepared and insensitive to His majesty. It is not shallow, superficial, or flippant. Worship is life lived in the presence of an infinitely righteous and omnipresent God by one utterly aware of His holiness and consequently overwhelmed with his own unholiness.

You and I may not have a vision of God like Isaiah's, but nonetheless, the lesson is true that when we enter into the presence of God, we must see Him as holy. And our sense of sinfulness and fear is proportional to our experience of the presence of God. If you have never worshiped God with a broken and a contrite spirit, you've never fully worshiped God, because that is the only appropriate response to entering the presence of Holy God.

My heartfelt concern is that there is too much shallowness today with regard to God's holiness. Our relationship to God has become too casual. In the modern mind, God has become almost human, so buddy-buddy that we don't understand His holy indignation against sin. If we burst into His presence with lives unattended to by repentance, confession, and cleansing by the Spirit, we are vulnerable to His holy reaction. It is only by His grace that we breathe each breath, is it not? He has every reason to take our lives, for the wages of our sin is death.

There is much supposed worship going on today that does not genuinely regard God as holy, and thus it falls woefully short. A lot of nice songs are being sung, nice feelings are being felt, nice thoughts are being thought, and nice emotions are being expressed, without a genuine acknowledgment of the holiness of God. That kind of worship bears no relationship to the worship we see in the Bible. It may be more psychological than theological, more fleshly than spiritual.

The response of a true worshiper to a vision of God is that, like Isaiah, he is overwhelmed with his own sinfulness and consequently consumed with a sense of holy terror. I am certain that if the people today who claim to have seen God really saw Him, they wouldn't be lining

up to get on the latest Christian talk show; they'd be
lying prostrate on the ground, grieving over their sin.

## REVERENCE AND GODLY FEAR

A true worshiper comes into the presence of God in
healthy fear. God punishes sin, even in those who are
redeemed. And He says in Hebrews 12:6, "Whom the
Lord loves, He disciplines, and He scourges every son
whom He receives."

Hebrews 12:28 goes on to say, "Let us have grace,
whereby we may serve God acceptably with reverence
and godly fear" (KJV). The word for *serve* is *latreuo*, a
word for worship. The writer is talking about acceptable
worship, and he lists two key elements: *reverence and
godly fear*. Note the reason he gives for such worship:
"For our God is a consuming fire" (v. 29).

*Reverence* carries a positive connotation. It describes a
sense of awe as we perceive the majesty of God. *Godly
fear*, on the other hand, can be seen as a sense of intimidation as we see the power and holiness of God, who "is
a consuming fire." That refers to His power to destroy,
His holy reaction against sin.

True worship, then, demands the sense of God's holiness, the sense of my sinfulness, and the cry for purging.
That's the essence of the proper attitude of worship. Let
me illustrate that principle from the life of Christ.

## THE RESPONSE TO JESUS

It seems to be difficult for Christians today to get away
from the idea that Jesus was a passive, amiable, meek-
and-mild being who walked through the world making
people feel good. Actually, when our Lord was here on
earth people were afraid of Him. It was overwhelming for
people to come face to face with the living God incarnate.
In fact, the normal reaction to Jesus from both believers
and skeptics was fear. He traumatized people.

Jesus' very presence was intimidating. Many things
contributed to that. His authority was apparent. "The
multitudes were amazed at His teaching, for He was

teaching as one having authority, and not as their scribes" (Matthew 7:28-29). His words were unique. "Never did a man speak the way this man speaks" (John 7:46). His works were undeniably of God. The blind man said, "If this man were not from God, He could do nothing" (John 9:33). His wisdom was superhuman. "No one was able to answer Him a word, nor did anyone dare from that day on to ask Him a another question" (Matthew 22:45). His purity was undeniable. He said, "Which one of you convicts Me of sin?" (John 8:46). His truthfulness was unquestionable. He challenged those who tried Him, "If I have spoken wrongly, bear witness of the wrong" (John 18:23). His power was astounding. He fed the multitude, cast out demons, and spoke to a fig tree, causing it to die on the spot.

Even when He was a boy the teachers were shocked when He spoke. His knowledge was beyond anything the people of His day had ever known, and John 7:15 says, "The Jews therefore were marveling, saying, 'How has this man become learned, having never been educated?' " His independence made religious leaders shudder. The Pharisees marveled that He didn't wash before dinner. He defied their ceremonies. His composure and confidence were beyond anything human.

You see, Jesus' presence aroused a sense of fear in people. He intimidated them. One of the reasons the Pharisees wanted to get rid of Him was that they could not handle that intimidation.

Perhaps the most striking reactions to Jesus were from those who saw the blazing revelation of His deity. Whether they believed or not, the reaction was the same; they were terrified.

Even the disciples were fearful when they faced squarely the reality that He was God. In Mark 4:37-41, we read that while the disciples were crossing the lake in a boat with Jesus, a storm struck, and their boat began to sink. The disciples panicked and awoke Jesus, who was sleeping through it all. He calmed the storm, and rebuked them for their unbelief, and verse 41 tells us that

they were "exceedingly" terrified. It's far more frighten-
ing to face the holiness of God inside your boat than to
have a storm outside your boat.

In the next chapter of Mark, Jesus encountered a man
possessed by a legion of demons. When Jesus sent the
demons into a herd of pigs and they went into the lake
and drowned, the people of the town came out and
pleaded with Him to leave their country (Mark 5:17). It
was not because they owned the pigs, or they would have
demanded compensation. Rather, they were terrified in
His holy presence. They knew God was in action, and
they were not willing to face their own sin before Jesus.

Later in Mark 5, we read that a crowd gathered around
Jesus. In the crowd was a lady who had been sick for
many years. She believed in her heart that Christ had so
much power that she could just grab hold of His robe and
be healed. She pushed her way through the crowd and
reached out in her feeble way and clung to His garment,
clutching it in her hand, and instantly she was healed.

Jesus said, "Who touched My garments?" Verse 33
says, "The woman fearing and trembling, aware of what
had happened to her, came and fell down before Him,
and told Him the whole truth." She knew she was in the
presence of God.

The word *trembling* is the word used in the Septuagint
to describe the shaking of Mount Sinai when God gave
the law. She really shook! She was terrified. A sinner in
the presence of the Holy God should be.

In Luke 5, Peter was fishing and couldn't catch anything. The Lord came along and told him where to let his
nets down, and he did, and Peter's catch was so great
that he couldn't haul it in. When he finally got help from
another boat to bring in the catch, there were so many
fish that both boats began to sink. It was a demonstration to Peter of Jesus' deity. Peter "fell down at Jesus'
feet, saying, 'Depart from me, for I am a sinful man, O
Lord' " (v. 8). All he could see was his own sinfulness
when confronted with the power and presence of Holy
God.

The true worshiper comes in that spirit. He is broken

over his sinfulness. A true worshiping life is a life of contrition; it is a life that sees sin and confesses continually (see 1 John 1:9). It seeks to hide at first, and then rather to be purged.

## GOD'S GRACE DOES NOT CANCEL HIS HOLINESS

Perhaps we have lost the fear of God because we take His grace for granted. At the very beginning, God said to Adam and Eve, "The day you eat from [the forbidden tree], you shall surely die" (Genesis 2:17). They ate from it, but they didn't die that day. God showed them grace.

Throughout the Bible we see that God is gracious. The law called for death for adulterers, blasphemers, and even rebellious children. But many in the Old Testament violated God's laws without suffering the death penalty the law prescribed. David committed adultery, but God didn't take his life. He was gracious.

And He continues to be gracious. We are alive only because God is merciful. But instead of our accepting the mercy of God with great thankfulness and keeping the perspective of fearing God, we begin to get used to it. Consequently, when God does punish sin, we think He's unjust.

People look at the Old Testament and question the goodness of God. Some have even suggested that we shouldn't teach the Bible to children because the God it speaks of is too violent. Why, they ask, would God command the Israelites to destroy all the people living in Canaan? What kind of God would snuff out the life of a man simply for touching the Ark? What kind of God would cause a bear to destroy a group of children for making fun of a prophet's baldness? What kind of God would open the ground and swallow up people? What kind of God would drown the whole world?

We are so used to mercy and grace that we think God has no right to be angry with sin. Romans 3:18 sums up the world's attitude: "There is no fear of God before their eyes."

Do you know why God took the lives of certain people in the Bible? It was not because they were more sinful than anyone else; it was because somewhere along the line in the long process of grace and mercy, God had to set some examples to make men fear. He turned Lot's wife into a pillar of salt, not because she did something worse than anyone else ever did, but because she was to be His example. First Corinthians 10 cites some Old Testament people who were destroyed, and verse 11 says, "Now these things happened to them as an example, and they were written for our instruction." The highway of history is paved with God's mercy and grace. But there are billboards all the way along, posted so that men may know that God at any moment has a right to take their lives.

God is gracious, but don't confuse His mercy with justice. God is not unjust when He acts in a holy manner against sin. Don't ever get to the place that you are so used to mercy and grace that you abuse it by going on in your sin. Or that you question God when He does what He has every right to do against a sinner. Don't abuse God's grace; He will judge you, too. But know this: He is holy, and He is to be feared.

THE REAL QUESTION

The question is not why God so dramatically judges some sinners, but rather why He lets any of us live. God has every right to punish sin, and "the wages of sin is death" (Romans 6:23). Lamentations 3:22 says, "It is of the Lord's mercies that we are not consumed, because his compassions fail not" (KJV).

God's mercy, however, is not His blessing on our sin. Most of us have been guilty of the same kind of sin of hypocrisy as Ananias and Sapphira. Or we have come to the Lord's table in an unworthy manner like those in Corinth who died for their sin. Or we have acted in a worldly fashion like Lot's wife, who was turned to a pillar of salt. The real question is not why God judged them so quickly and harshly, but why He hasn't done the same with us.

One reason for God's mercy is that He is driving us to repentance. Romans 2:4 says, "The kindness of God

leads you to repentance." God, by His mercy and kindness to us, is often actually bringing us to the point
where we see His love for us and our need of repentance.

*The Chronicles of Narnia*, a series of children's books
by C. S. Lewis, are a fantasy based on the truths of Christianity. Aslan, the golden lion, represents Christ. And in
his description of that fierce and loving lion, Lewis has
given evidence of a remarkable understanding of Christ's
character.

In one scene, some talking beavers are describing
Aslan to Lucy, Susan, and Peter, who are newcomers to
the realm of Narnia. In anticipation of meeting him, they
ask questions that reveal their fears.

> "Ooh!" said Susan, "I'd thought he was a man. Is he—
> quite safe? I shall feel rather nervous about meeting a
> lion."
> "That you will, dearie, and no mistake," said Mrs.
> Beaver, "if there's anyone who can appear before
> Aslan without their knees knocking, they're either
> braver than most or else just silly."
> "Then he isn't safe?" said Lucy.
> "Safe?" said Mr. Beaver. "Don't you hear what Mrs.
> Beaver tells you? Who said anything about safe?
> 'Course he isn't safe. But he's good. He's the King, I tell
> you."[1]

After the children met Aslan, Lucy observed that his
paws were potentially very soft or very terrible. They
could be as soft as velvet with his claws drawn in, or
sharp as knives with his claws extended.

We in modern Christianity have somehow missed that
truth. While we are thankful for the reality of His grace,
and while we want to enjoy the experience of His love, we
have somehow neglected the truth of His holiness. And it
is eating at the heart of our worship.

1. C. S. Lewis, *The Lion, the Witch, and the Wardrobe* (New
   York: MacMillan, 1950), pp. 75-76. Copyright 1950 by the
   Trustees of the Estate of C. S. Lewis, renewed 1978 by
   Arthur Owen Barfield. Used by permission.

God is a living, eternal, glorious, merciful, holy being. His worshipers must come in the contrition and humility and brokenness of sinners who see ourselves against the backdrop of that holiness. And that should put such thanksgiving and joy in our hearts for the gift of His forgiveness that our worship is all it should be.

We are to live lives of confession, repentance, and turning from our sin so that our worship is that which fully pleases God. We dare not go rushing into His presence in unholiness. We cannot worship God acceptably except with reverence and godly fear, and in the beauty of holiness. We must return to the biblical teaching of God's utter and awesome holiness in order to be filled with the gratitude and humility that characterize true worship.

# 8

# A New Era Dawns

To bring all this glorious theology of worship into concise and practical terms, we turn to the account of Jesus' conversation with the Samaritan woman as recorded in John 4. There we have the privilege of learning the meaning of worship from the very One whom we worship.

At least ten times in that simple account, some form of the most frequently used Greek word for "worship" (*proskuneo*) appears. Thus the idea of worship clearly dominates the passage; and although it is brief, it contains all the essential elements of worship in embryonic form. It is the most definitive, the most important, and the clearest teaching on the theme of worship in all the New Testament. It will be our focus for a few chapters.

We have seen already that worship is not merely an activity to be injected into our schedules at certain intervals; rather, worship is itself a whole-life commitment, an all-encompassing response to Holy God, possible only for those who have been redeemed. We have suggested a definition of worship and examined the importance of worship, the nature of worship, and the object of worship. The account in John 4 brings all that together and sheds even more light on the subject.

A DIVINE APPOINTMENT

John describes the events that led up to Jesus' conversation with the Samaritan woman:

> He left Judea, and departed again into Galilee. And He had to pass through Samaria. So He came to a city of Samaria, called Sychar, near the parcel of ground that Jacob gave to his son Joseph; and Jacob's well was there. Jesus therefore being wearied from His journey, was sitting thus by the well. It was about the sixth hour. There came a woman of Samaria to draw water. Jesus said to her, "Give Me a drink." For His disciples had gone away into the city to buy food. [John 4:3-9]

Although the route north was most direct if the traveler went through Samaria, the fact that Jesus went that way was unusual, for normally Jews would go many miles out of their way to avoid the Samaritans, whom they considered unclean.

But Jesus was in Samaria for a specific purpose. His journey there was not incidental; it was planned, ordained by God. The King James Version says, "He must needs go through Samaria" (v. 4). He had a divine appointment with a special woman. God was seeking her to be a true worshiper, and He sent Jesus to bring her into that special relationship.

A HOUSE DIVIDED

Actually the Samaritans, who were of mixed descent, had their roots in the ancient nation of Israel. The people of that land had been united under Saul, David, and Solomon. When the kingdom split, the southern kingdom—Judah—became independent. Eventually, the northern kingdom—Israel—guilty of terrifying wickedness, was divinely judged. In 721 B.C. Israel was defeated by Sargon. Most of the people were taken captive to Assyria, where they became the slaves of the Assyrians. The only ones allowed to remain in the land were the poor. (They were a liability, representing welfare cases to the Assyrians, so they were left behind.) Foreigners from surrounding areas, particularly from Babylon, began to move into Israel. They intermarried with those remaining Jews. The race that developed as a result was known as the Samaritans, named for their capital city of Samaria. They were despised by the Jews as those who had "sold their birthright."

Their religion became a hybrid of Judaism and paganism. History indicates that they seemed to want to maintain their Jewish heritage, even begging the Jews for a priest who would teach them the true worship of God, but they were rejected in their request.

And so they were left in their syncretistic religion. The only alternative was to establish their own place of worship. They built a temple on Mount Gerizim and began to worship in their own way, apart from Judaism.

That situation lasted until 128 B.C., when a Maccabean ruler, John Hyrcanus, destroyed the Samaritans' temple. It was never rebuilt. They simply continued worshiping on Mount Gerizim. And to this day, although there are fewer than five hundred Samaritans left on the face of the earth, they gather regularly on that vacant mountain and carry out their unique, ceremonial, sacrificial worship, independent of Jerusalem.

## IS THIS NOT THE CHRIST?

In the days of our Lord, the Samaritans were despised, looked down on, hated by the Jews, who had no dealings with them at all. That explains why the Samaritan woman was surprised that Jesus, a Jew, would stop at the well and speak to her:

> The Samaritan woman therefore said to Him, "How is it that You, being a Jew, ask me for a drink since I am a Samaritan woman?" (For Jews have no dealings with Samaritans.) Jesus answered and said to her, "If you knew the gift of God, and who it is who says to you, 'Give Me a drink,' you would have asked Him, and He would have given you living water." She said to Him, "Sir, You have nothing to draw with and the well is deep; where then do you get that living water?

You are not greater than our father Jacob, are You,
who gave us the well and drank of it himself, and his
sons, and his cattle?" Jesus answered and said to her,
"Everyone who drinks of this water shall thirst again;
but whoever drinks of the water that I shall give him
shall never thirst; but the water that I shall give him
shall become in him a well of water springing up to
eternal life." [vv. 7-14]

Thus Jesus offered her the gift of eternal life, and His
claims excited her curiosity. She may have been somewhat confused about what He was saying, but she knew
it was something spiritually profound—she understood
that He was not speaking of literal water. People in that
part of the world were accustomed to parables. It was not
unusual—especially for a teacher or rabbi— to talk in terminology that drew spiritual meaning from life's sur-
roundings and situations. The woman's response to
Jesus, in the same terms as His analogy, comes in verse
15, "Sir, give me this water, so I will not be thirsty, nor
come all the way here to draw."
Then Jesus further penetrated her heart, saying,

"Go, call your husband, and come here." The woman
answered and said, "I have no husband." Jesus said
to her, "You have well said, 'I have no husband'; for
you have had five husbands, and the one whom you
now have is not your husband; this you have said
truly." [vv. 16-19]

If there was any question in her mind whether He was
a man of God, it vanished after that amazing revelation.
Her response is recorded in verse 19: "Sir, I perceive that
you are a prophet." She saw in Christ omniscience in
action. There could be no other explanation for a
stranger's having such knowledge.
Although the Samaritans accepted only the Pentateuch
as revelation from God, it had enough truth about Messiah to lead them to anticipate Him. The power of Jesus'
personage must have caused the woman to see Him for
what He was, for she later told the men of the city,

"Come, see a man who told me all the things that I have done; this is not the Christ, is it?" (John 4:29).

Jesus had isolated the sin in her life, and that caused her to consider seriously whether He might be the Messiah. She sensed His supernaturalness for two obvious reasons. First, He brought a message of spiritual truth, and second, He knew what was humanly impossible for Him to know. He had a divine message and divine perception.

Recognizing that He was sent from God, she asked Him the most pertinent religious question she knew: "Our fathers worshiped in this mountain, and you people say that in Jerusalem is the place where men ought to worship." In other words, "Who is right? The Jews or the Samaritans? What is the proper way to worship?"

Jesus said to her, "Woman, believe Me, an hour is coming when neither in this mountain, nor in Jerusalem, shall you worship the Father. You worship that which you do not know. We worship that which we know, for salvation is from the Jews. But an hour is coming, and now is, when the true worshipers shall worship the Father in spirit and truth; for such people the Father seeks to be His worshipers. God is spirit, and those who worship Him must worship in spirit and truth." [vv. 20-24]

Behind her question was more than just theological curiosity. She seemed to have a genuine desire to know and experience God's forgiving, cleansing grace for her sin, but she did not know where to go for it. Like many, she associated worship with a place.

EVERYONE DID WHAT WAS RIGHT IN HIS OWN EYES

Her confusion was understandable, for she lived amid two totally differing systems of worship, neither of which seemed to offer the kind of satisfying spiritual life Jesus was talking about. Jewish worship was highly ritualized, performed according to strict liturgy, with very firm biblical and traditional rules for how and when and with whom it should be done. Samaritan worship, on the other hand, was not quite as elaborate, ornate, and sophisticated.

Jesus' answer must have stunned her, because He implied that both groups were offering unacceptable worship. As we shall see in chapter 11, both Jews and Samaritans were guilty of shallow, indifferent, self-styled worship, not according to the will of God.

Jesus told the woman that the Jewish mode of worship and the Samaritan mode of worship were to be eliminated totally in favor of the divine method of genuine, spiritual worship: "Woman, believe Me, an hour is coming when neither in this mountain, nor in Jerusalem, shall you worship the Father . . . The true worshipers shall worship the Father in Spirit and in truth" (vv. 21-23).

### SOMETHING OLD, SOMETHING NEW

Jesus' statement can be interpreted several ways. Jesus could have been predicting the woman's conversion, saying, "You're about to enter into a relationship with God through Me that's going to make it so you don't worship God in either place, but in your heart." And certainly that was included in His meaning.

But taken in their widest possible significance, Jesus' words imply, "I will bring about redemptive work on the cross of Calvary, and that will eliminate for all true worshipers everything that is in any way associated with the Old Covenant, whether genuine or false."

The point is that an end to the old ceremonial systems of worship was coming very fast, for her and everyone else. Jesus said in verse 23: "An hour is coming, and now is." Those are fascinating words. In essence, Jesus was saying, "I'm standing in the transition, and in one hand I have the Old Covenant and in the other hand I have the New Covenant. The hour is coming (and it's already here because I am here) when the current system of law and sacrifice and ritual will be gone and the New Covenant will come." He was clearly predicting the end of the external ceremonial system.

The end of the Old Covenant came as He promised.

God dramatized it marvelously with one great climactic event, which occurred when Jesus died on the cross. The veil of the Temple was torn from the top to the bottom, signifying that God had ended the whole system. The Holy of Holies was exposed. Access to God was open to all. The shadows gave way to the substance (cf. Colossians 2:16-17). And just to make sure no one was confused about the status of the old system, in A.D. 70 God allowed Jerusalem and the Temple to be destroyed. It has never been rebuilt.

The New Testament book of Hebrews tells us that because of what Christ has done we have a new *kind* of worship. Hebrews 10:19-20 says, "Therefore, brethren, we have confidence to enter the holy place by the blood of Jesus, *by a new and living way* which He inaugurated for us" (emphasis added).

The theme of Hebrews 10 is the inadequacy of the Old Covenant system. Verse 4 says, "For it is impossible for the blood of bulls and goats to take away sins." The sacrificial system couldn't deal conclusively with sins. Its offerings were temporary symbols, and they were constantly repeated. Verse 11 describes the problem: "And every priest stands daily ministering and offering time after time the same sacrifices, which can never take away sins."

What a contrast we see in the work of Jesus Christ: "But He, having offered one sacrifice for sins for all time, sat down at the right hand of God" (v. 12). He sat down because His work was finished.

> For by one offering He has perfected for all time those who are sanctified . . . "This is the [new] covenant that I will make with them after those days, says the Lord: I will put My laws upon their heart, and upon their mind I will write them . . . and their sins and their lawless deeds I will remember no more." Now where there is forgiveness of these things, there is no longer any offering for sin. [vv. 14-18]

So the sacrificial system was over when Christ died. He perfected everything. The ceremonial system, with its sacrifices, Sabbath observances, and ritual worship, was abolished forever.

## WHAT ABOUT THE SABBATH?

The sacrifices are gone, yet there are those who teach that even today we should observe the seventh day of the week as the Sabbath. Acceptable worship, they say, is not possible for those who fail to keep the Saturday Sabbath. That contradicts the clear teaching of this passage and others in God's Word.

It is true that under the Old Covenant in Israel, all worship revolved around the Sabbath. The Jewish calendar operated in cycles of seven, and all the days of worship, all the great feasts, festivals, and celebrations were tied to the Sabbath concept.

There were several kinds of Sabbaths, but they all had one purpose—cessation of labor to worship God. Leviticus 23:3 describes the weekly Sabbath, "For six days, work may be done; but on the seventh day there is a sabbath of complete rest, a holy convocation." The rest of the chapter describes the many other Sabbath feast days and celebrations, each of which was a holy convocation, a sacred time when the people of God came together for worship.

In Leviticus 25, God outlines instructions for two more kinds of Sabbath observances—the year-long sabbath that was to be observed every seventh year, when the fields were not to be planted and the people were to concentrate on worship for a year; and the year of jubilee, which was to occur every fiftieth year, or at the conclusion of seven sabbath years. In the year of jubilee, the ultimate Sabbath observance came in the seventh month on the Day of Atonement. On that day a trumpet was sounded and all slaves, prisoners, and refugees were freed; property that had been bought was returned to its original owner; and everyone returned to his own family.

The fundamental concepts behind every Sabbath observance were rest and worship. The weekly Sabbath was a rest for the people from the labors of daily life and a time to focus on God. The Sabbath feasts were special

holy days set aside for worship and reflection on the
things of God. The seventh-year Sabbaths allowed even
the fields to rest for an entire year. And the year of jubilee
set slaves and captives free and provided rest and cele-
bration for everyone.

The Sabbath purpose was purely *symbolic*. In the
same way that the sacrificial system with all its spotless
lambs and slain bullocks and blood sacrifices symbolized
the atonement Christ made on the cross, the Sabbath
system symbolized the true rest and true worship for the
people of God to be found through Messiah. The Sabbath
system pointed to a time when God's people would unite
in a holy convocation, a spiritual liberating of captives
and setting free of slaves—a real cessation of labor. It
looked forward to the coming of the New Covenant.

Jesus Himself announced the arrival of that reality. In
Luke 4, we read that He went to the synagogue on the
Sabbath, picked up the scroll, and read,

> The Spirit of the Lord is upon Me,
> Because He anointed Me to preach the gospel to the
>    poor.
> He has sent Me to proclaim release to the captives,
> And recovery of sight to the blind,
> To set free those who are downtrodden,
> To proclaim the favorable [jubilee] year of the Lord.
>                                              vv. 18-19

The language of that passage from Isaiah is exactly like
that which Moses prescribed for the Day of Atonement
Sabbath in the year of jubilee (Leviticus 25:10). When
Jesus had read that much of the passage,

> He closed the book, and gave it back to the attendant,
> and sat down; and the eyes of all in the synagogue
> were fixed upon Him. And He began to say to them,
> "Today this Scripture has been fulfilled in your hear-
> ing." [vv. 20-21]

In other words, Jesus Himself claimed to be the fulfillment of all that was symbolized in the year of jubilee. It
was a monumental moment in redemptive history.

He proclaimed, "Come to Me, all who are weary and heavy-laden, and I will give you rest" (Matthew 11:28). It was an offer of an abiding Sabbath rest. He was the fulfillment of all that the Sabbaths pictured. And we don't need the picture if we have the reality. Sabbaths are no more a part of the New Covenant than animal sacrifices are.

That is exactly the reason Jesus felt free to violate all the Jewish Sabbath ordinances. If He wanted to travel on the Sabbath, He traveled. He plucked corn and ate it on the Sabbath. He healed on the Sabbath. And He did it openly, knowing that it would bring about a confrontation. In fact, He claimed lordship over the entire sabbatical system, and He was not afraid to ignore Jewish rules and regulations. Why should He be? He was the substance of which the Sabbaths were merely shadows.

Paul comes to that very conclusion in Colossians 2:16-17:

> Let no one act as your judge in regard to food or drink or in respect to a festival or a new moon or a Sabbath day—things which are a mere shadow of what is to come; but the substance belongs to Christ.

We worship under a new system, not the dead way of animal sacrifice, not the old way of Sabbaths and ceremonies, "but a new and living way, which He inaugurated for us through the veil, that is, His flesh, and since we have a great priest over the house of God, let us draw near" (Hebrews 10:20). External ceremonies, forms, and special days are not binding any longer. All this marvelous truth was bound up in the pregnant words of our Lord as He answered the Samaritan woman. (See also Romans 14:5-6.)

Not Much Has Changed

We live today under the New Covenant. But is the worship of today any better than that encountered by Jesus at His first advent? If Jesus were to arrive on the scene today I wonder what He would have to say about modern worship that purports to be in His name.

In his book *Worship*, A. P. Gibbs describes the false, heavily ritualistic worship of many contemporary churches:

> Much of the so-called "public worship" in Christendom, is merely a form of Christianized Judaism, and, in some cases, thinly veiled paganism. . . . In Judaism there was a separate priestly caste who alone could conduct the worship of Israel. In Christendom a man-made priesthood called "the clergy," is essential to its worship, in spite of the plain teaching of the New Testament that all believers are priests. These priests of Judaism wore a distinctive dress, as also does the clergy. Judaism emphasized an earthly sanctuary, or building. In like manner, Christendom makes much of its consecrated "places of worship," and miscalls the edifice "a church," and refers to it as "the house of God." Jewish priests had an altar on which were offered sacrifices to God. Christendom has erected "altars" in these ornate buildings, before which candles burn and incense is offered and, in many cases, on which a wafer is kept, which is looked upon as the body of Christ! It is hardly necessary to say that all this copying of Judaism is absolutely foreign to the teaching of the New Testament.
>
> Thus Christendom has initiated its own specially educated and ordained priesthood, whose presence is indispensable to "administer the sacraments." These men, robed in gorgeous vestments, from within a roped off "sanctuary," stand before a bloodless "altar," with a background of burning candles, crosses and smoking incense, and "conduct the worship" for the laity. With the use of an elaborate prepared ritual, with stereotyped prayers, and responses from the audience, the whole service proceeds smoothly and with mechanical precision. It is a marvel of human invention and ingenuity, with an undoubted appeal to the esthetic; but a tragic and sorry substitute for the spiritual worship

which our Lord declared that His Father sought from His redeemed children.[1]

If our Lord came today He would denounce that kind of ritualistic worship. He would rebuke the Sabbath keepers. He would also impugn the less formal worship of many evangelical churches, which is more like Samaritan worship—not as ritualistic, but nevertheless, often external, superficial, ignorant, or wrongly motivated and thus unacceptable.

Christ ushered in the new era of true worship—worship that does not focus on the externals or on the symbolic but on the internal and genuine. That is what the Father seeks, and that is what the Son demands. Anything less falls short.

1. A. P. Gibbs, *Worship* (Kansas City:Walterick, n.d.), pp. 97-98.

# 9

# This Must Be the Place

When Jesus said something to someone on a one-to-one basis, it was surely difficult to evade. The woman at the well was visibly affected by the realization that Jesus knew her sin. Her conscience was pricked. Her soul was pierced. She was unmasked as an adulteress. She knew she was a covenant breaker—a stranger to the things of God.

In spite of her sinful life, the woman's response to Christ proved she had an open heart. And the realization that she was apart from truth, apart from life, and apart from righteousness, began to dawn on her heart and mind. She felt a heavy weight of conviction, and her immediate reaction to His words was a desire to set things right. Her first thought was of worship to God, and she asked Jesus to tell her where—in Mount Gerizim or in Jerusalem. The Jews were in Jerusalem worshiping their way. The Samaritans were on Gerizim worshiping their way. Which group was doing it right?

As we have intimated, the woman's confusion grew out of her society's shallow perspective, which led to the belief that worship is something you do at a prescribed place at a set time in a ritualistic manner. And she wasn't sure what place was the right place. So she asked Jesus. He told her that soon there would not be an "up here" and a "down there." Worship is not an activity to be confined to a specific place, time, and form.

## WHAT ABOUT THE TEMPLE?

Jesus' answer raises some interesting questions. First of all, we might ask if the place of worship is of any concern at all. What was the purpose of the Temple? If worship was not to be confined to a place, why was a place of worship built? And why do we worship in a church building?

One thing we have seen to be clear from Jesus' words: the old system is dead. The place of worship is not in Mount Gerizim, and it is not the Temple at Jerusalem. The old ceremonial rituals and observances are gone. There is no place today for an elite priesthood, altars, sacrificial masses, burning candles, or smoking incense. Those things are Judaism and paganism dragged across the line between covenants, ignoring the new and living way and the priesthood of all believers.

It is essential to understand that the Temple was only a resident symbol to stimulate worship as a way of life. If you don't comprehend that you miss the whole point of the Temple. Temples are symbols, not realities, just like the sacrifices and the Sabbath system were symbolic of greater realities. The woman needed to understand that and so do we.

## LIVING TEMPLES

What new reality takes the place of the Temple of the Old Testament? Paul wrote about one aspect of it to the Corinthian church: "Do you not know that your body is a temple of the Holy Spirit who is in you?" (1 Corinthians 6:19).

Every believer is a living, breathing temple in which God dwells. That means believers can worship anywhere, at any time—God goes with them in an abiding presence. A Christian can worship Him at the beach, in the mountains, driving down the road, sitting under a tree, walking in the woods, running in the country, sitting in the living room, in a church building, or anywhere under any kind of circumstance or condition. The sphere of worship is unlimited.

In Hebrews 10:19, after those wonderful statements about the offering of Jesus Christ, which sanctifies us once for all, and the New Covenant, which gives us access to God, we read these words: "Therefore, brethren, we have confidence to enter the holy place by the blood of Jesus, by a new and living way."

That is the supreme reality of worship. God has permitted us to enter into the Holy of Holies through the blood of Christ. Such a thing could not be done by those living under the Old Covenant. They worshiped God from a distance.

You who believe in the New Covenant have been forever brought near. Christ went to the cross and offered Himself in order to give you access to worship God freely—to bring you into the Holy of Holies. The invitation is ever open, as the writer to the Hebrews emphasized: "Let us draw near with a sincere heart in full assurance of faith, having our hearts sprinkled clean from an evil conscience and our bodies washed with pure water" (Hebrews 10:22). James echoed that truth when he wrote, "Draw near to God and He will draw near to you" (James 4:8).

We have been saved in order that the way to God might be open. We may go into the Holy of Holies and draw near with a true heart, knowing that we are welcome there through the new and living way—anywhere, any time.

So, in one sense, we do not have to come to a church building to worship God—but there is another dimension.

A WORSHIPING COMMUNITY

Hebrews 10 goes on: "And let us consider how to stimulate one another to love and good deeds, not forsaking our own assembling together" (vv. 24-25). As believers, we are to assemble to stimulate one another to love (that's sharing) and to good deeds (that's doing good). Remember that both of those activities constitute worship (see chapter 2).

Worshiping God is not really a geographical issue, but that doesn't rule out congregational worship, and it doesn't mean a building cannot be specially designated for worship. In fact, even under the New Covenant, God has a temple, apart from the temple of our individual bodies, where He meets with His people. It is a very special building. Paul describes it in Ephesians 2:19-22:

> So then you are no longer strangers and aliens, but you are fellow citizens with the saints, and are of God's household, having been built upon the foundation of the apostles and prophets, Christ Jesus Himself being the corner stone, in whom the whole building, being fitted together is growing into a holy temple in the Lord; in whom you also are being built together into a dwelling of God in the Spirit.

All believers are linked together as fellow citizens in the kingdom of light. All who know Christ belong to the household of God. The church is a family, linked by common citizenship and common life. But there is more. As believers, we are a building, built on the foundation of the apostles and the prophets, and Jesus Christ Himself is the chief cornerstone. We are a temple, fitted together and growing—the dwelling place of God through the Spirit.

That does not negate the truth that each believer's body is also a temple of the Holy Spirit. But in a larger sense, the visible, living assembly of the redeemed saints becomes the larger temple of God in the Holy Spirit. In 1 Corinthians 6:19, when Paul wrote of believers as temples, he had in mind individual believers. But three chapters earlier, in 1 Corinthians 3:16, when he wrote, "Do you not know that you are a temple of God?", the noun he used for "you" is plural. He was speaking in a collective sense, of the community of saints, as God's dwelling place.

Second Corinthians 6:16 says: "We are the temple of

the living God; just as God said, 'I will dwell in them and walk among them.' " God moves in the midst of the community of saints when the church comes together. The church is His unique dwelling place—more real than the symbolic Old Testament edifices—a temple God blesses with His wonderful presence.

First Peter 2:5 says: "You also, as living stones, are built up as a spiritual house for a holy priesthood, to offer up spiritual sacrifices acceptable to God through Jesus Christ." That is a description of worship. The church is not a building made with stone. It is a building made with living flesh. We believers are living stones in God's temple, and when we come together we constitute a place of worship where God manifests Himself in ways that He cannot manifest Himself when we are alone. Believers become the living temple of God, offering to Him spiritual sacrifices not possible anywhere other than in the assembly of the redeemed church.

## NOT STYLE, BUT SUBSTANCE

Corporate worship is not what most people think it is. Many people understand worship in the church as a casual to formal activity that takes place once a week. Worship is often seen as the form, the style, rather than the substance. But what is true in our individual lives under the New Covenant is also true in the corporate assembly of believers: worship is not primarily an external activity.

Neither is worship stimulated by gimmicks. People have suggested to me that we should place signs around our church building that say "Quiet!", or, "Keep Silence in the Place of Worship." Some churches insert a notice in the bulletin telling people not to talk when they come in. And I suppose some would have the pastor put bells on his suit so that when he comes into the service like the priest of old and you hear the tinkle you know it's time to get holy.

That has nothing to do with real worship. Worship is not energized by artificial methods. If you feel you must have formalized ritual, or a certain kind of mood music to worship, what you do isn't worship. Music and liturgy can assist or express a worshiping heart, but they cannot make a non-worshiping heart into a worshiping one. The danger is that they can give a non-worshiping heart the sense of having worshiped.

So the crucial factor in worship in the church is not the form of worship, but the state of the hearts of the saints. If our corporate worship isn't the expression of our individual worshiping lives, it is unacceptable. If you think you can live anyway you want and then go to church on Sunday morning and turn on worship with the saints, you're wrong.

Worship does not occur in a vacuum. As believers, we are responsible to the rest of the church to maintain a consistent life-style of genuine, acceptable worship. Our failure to do so will adversely affect the rest of the Body of Christ, just as Achan's sin had disastrous effects on the whole nation of Israel. What we do throughout the week will affect the members of the church with whom we worship on Sunday.

WORSHIP IS GIVING

The regular coming together of the saints is an essential element in the new and living way of worship. When the redeemed assemble with hearts overflowing with praise, cultivated through life-styles of pure, acceptable worship, together the congregation is mutually stimulated to worship God. There should be a bursting out, a boiling over, of true praise and heartfelt worship, because what has been enjoyed individually is expressed, then enriched and enhanced when brought into the joy of the assembly. The results are powerful.

Why do you go to church? When you meet together with the saints, is it really for worship? Or do you go to church for what you can get out of it? Do you come away having scrutinized the soloist, analyzed the choir, and criticized the message?

We've been too long conditioned to think that the church is to entertain us. That is not the case. Soren Kierkegaard said, "People have the idea that the preacher is an actor on a stage and they are the critics, blaming or praising him. What they don't know is that they are the actors on the stage; he is merely the prompter standing in the wings, reminding them of their lost lines." And God is the audience!

It is not unusual to hear someone say, "I didn't get anything out of church." My response is, "What did you give God? How was your heart prepared to give?"

If you go to church selfishly to seek a blessing, you have missed the point of worship. We go to give glory, not to get blessed. An understanding of that will effect how you critique the church experience. The issue isn't, Did I get anything out of it? but, Did I from my heart give glory to God? Since blessing comes from God in response to worship, if you aren't blessed, it isn't usually because of poor music or preaching (though they may occasionally prove to be insurmountable obstacles), but because of a selfish heart that does not give God glory.

SYMBIOSIS

Although it is intensely personal, there is nothing self-centered about genuine worship. If believers are to maintain a consistent life-style of continuous worship, they need the fellowship and encouragement of other believers as they assemble for group worship. Individual worship and corporate worship feed each other. So on the one hand, I need the fellowship of the saints. On the other hand, the community of saints needs me to live a consistent life of worship.

The source of most of the problems people have in their Christian lives relates to two things: either they are not worshiping six days a week with their life, or they are not worshiping one day a week with the assembly of the saints. We need both.

If you go to church only when it is convenient, you will never be victorious and productive as a Christian. You can't succeed on your own; you need to have the spiritual stimulation of fellow believers. We live in such an easy-come, easy-go, casual, flippant society that people don't make consistent, faithful commitments, and then they wonder why they fail. The answer is clear. Spiritual success requires commitment to others.

We don't need sacrifices, and we don't need priests. The sacrifice has once for all been offered. We have immediate access to God on our own. But we need the living stones laid one upon the other that constitute the habitation of the living God.

A pastor went to see a man who didn't attend church very faithfully. The man was sitting before a fire, watching the warm glow of the coals. It was a cold winter day, but the coals were red hot, and the fire was warm. The pastor pleaded with the man to be more faithful in meeting with the people of God, but the man didn't seem to be getting the message.

So the pastor took the tongs beside the fireplace, pulled open the screen, and reached in and began to separate all the coals. When none of the coals was touching the others, he stood and watched in silence. In a matter of moments, they were all cold. "That's what's happening in your life," he told the man. "As soon as you isolate yourself from God's people, the fire goes out." The man got the message.

The church is not the brick-and-mortar building in which the assembly meets; it is God's people in whom He dwells. In the church—among God's people, the true worshipers—we must bring a worshiping heart to stimulate others while being stimulated to love and good works. As that stimulation affects our souls we do good and share. The cycle is complete when we live out the overflow of praise and a continual heart of thanksgiving. Then worship is a way of life. For that we were redeemed.

# 10

# Worship the Father

The terminology Jesus employed to speak of God to the Samaritan woman in John 4 is significant. His entire discourse on the subject of worship focused on the importance of an appropriate response to a proper understanding of the nature of God. The location of worship is no longer the main concern, He told the woman. The issue is not *where* you worship, but rather *whom* you worship and *how* you worship.

In speaking to the woman at the well, Jesus used two nouns to refer to the "whom" of worship—*Father* and *spirit*—and both are essential in identifying the only legitimate object of true worship.

In earlier chapters, we looked closely at some of God's attributes. We saw that God is a personal, spiritual, trinitarian being who is unchanging, all-powerful, everywhere present, all-knowing, and holy. In the context of John 4, Jesus summarizes all of that for the woman at the well, and puts it in these terms: the true worshiper must perceive God as the Father and as spirit.

We have already discussed the fact that God is an immortal, invisible, and omnipresent spirit (see chapter 4). He cannot be seen or touched, and He cannot be repre-

sented by an idol or any kind of likeness. So worship
offered to Him must be spiritual worship.

But a worshiper may have the concept of a holy,
omnipotent, omnipresent, loving, righteous God who is a
spirit, and still fall short of worshiping the true God. The
most all-encompassing and clearest distinguishing characteristic of the true God is found in the title Jesus used
for God more often than any other—*Father.*

*Father* was Jesus' favorite title for God. The gospels
record about seventy times when Jesus spoke to God,
and every time He called Him Father, except when He
was on the cross, bearing the judgment for man's sin.
Then He said, "My God, My God, why hast Thou forsaken Me?" (Matthew 27:46).

WORSHIP THE FATHER

Three times in John 4, Jesus spoke of worshiping "the
Father." In John 4:21 we read, "worship the Father." In
the middle of verse 23, we read, "worship the Father."
And at the end of verse 23, "the Father seeketh such to
worship Him."

The concept of the fatherhood of God is normally misunderstood. When we think of God as Father, we usually
think of God as *our* loving Father. We are His children
and He is our Father, and we worship Him not only as a
vast, omnipresent, eternal, omniscient spirit, but also as
an intimate, loving, personal Father. And God is all
those things. But only once does Jesus refer to God as
"our Father" and that was not a direct address to God,
but a sample prayer, as the content of the prayer shows,
for Jesus would not have asked for forgiveness (Matthew
6:9). Several times in that same chapter Jesus refers to
God as "your Father," speaking of the disciples. So it is
right to think of God as *our* Father.

But in John 4, and all other times in the New Testament, when Jesus refers to God as "the Father," He is
not speaking of God's fatherhood in relationship to
believers. Whenever He used the term, Jesus' reference
was to God the Father's position in the Trinity, particularly as it relates to Him, the Son.

## How Is God Jesus' Father?

By acknowledging God as His Father, Jesus was not saying that He had an origin or a line of descent. The point of the Father-Son relationship within the Trinity is not that Jesus descends from God the Father, or that He was generated by or had His origin in Him. Jesus is an eternal being, descended from no one.

Neither is our Lord referring primarily to His submission to the Father's will. Although the elements of authority and submission enter into their Father-Son relationship, that is not its main emphasis.

Rather, the significance of the relationship between them is that the Son is of the same essence, of the same nature, as the Father. Jesus' use of the title was to express equality of deity. A father and son share the same nature and characteristics. When Jesus said that God was His Father, He was claiming to be equal with God, and the Jews of His day correctly understood the meaning of His words.

In John 5:17 we read Jesus' answer to the Jews who were persecuting Him for what He did on the Sabbath day: "My Father is working until now, and I Myself am working." How did they understand His words? Verse 18 tells us, "The Jews were seeking all the more to kill Him, because He not only was breaking the Sabbath, but also was calling God His own Father, making Himself equal with God."

And that was indeed exactly what He was saying. He was speaking of His and the Father's equality of being, essence, nature, and deity. Jesus is God, as surely as the Father is God, and when Jesus called Him Father, His meaning was clear to those who heard Him.

In John 10:29, Jesus says, "My Father, who has given them to Me, is greater than all; and no one is able to snatch them out of the Father's hand." Then He goes one step further in verse 30: "I and My Father are one."

The next verse tells us that the Jews took up stones to stone Him.

Jesus answered them, "I showed you many good

works from the Father; for which of them are you ston-
ing Me?'' The Jews answered Him, "For a good work
we do not stone You, but for blasphemy; and because
You, being a man, make Yourself out to be God." [vv.
32-33]

When Jesus said God was His Father, they knew He
meant that He shared God's essence. He was asserting
deity, affirming that He was equal to the sovereign, holy
God.

John 17 records Jesus' great prayer to the Father the
night He was arrested. He begins:

"Father, the hour has come; glorify Thy Son, that the
Son may glorify Thee, even as Thou gavest Him
authority over all mankind, that to all whom Thou
hast given Him, He may give eternal life. And this is
eternal life, that they may know Thee, the only true
God, and Jesus Christ whom Thou hast sent." [vv. 1-3]

Thus He again equates Himself with the Father and
says that eternal life is in knowing Him as much as it is
in knowing God. In verse 5 He says: "And now, glorify
Thou Me together with Thyself, Father, with the glory
which I had with Thee before the world was." That is a
clear statement that Jesus and God the Father are and
always have been equal.

In Matthew 11:27 we read that Jesus said, "All things
have been handed over to Me by My Father; and no one
knows the Son, except the Father; nor does any one
know the Father, except the Son; and anyone to whom
the Son wills to reveal Him." The Lord is repeating the
unique essential oneness of the Father and the Son.
There is an intimacy of knowledge between the Father
and the Son not available to any human perception.

In John 14:9, Jesus tells His disciples, "He who has
seen Me has seen the Father." That is the sum of the
truth of Jesus' teaching that He is the Son of God. Every
time He called God His Father, it was a blatant, outright
statement of His deity, His equality with God.

THE GOD AND FATHER OF OUR LORD JESUS

That God is distinctively identified as the Father of the
Lord Jesus is an important truth, often emphasized in
the Scriptures. In Ephesians 1 Paul wrote one of the great
paeans of praise in the Bible. In fact, from verse 3 to verse
14 is one long sentence of praise, and it begins this way
in verse 3: "Blessed be the God and Father of our Lord
Jesus Christ."

In verse 17 of the same chapter, Paul prays to "the God
of our Lord Jesus Christ, the Father of glory." Paul is
careful always to identify God with the Lord Jesus
Christ. Second Corinthians 1:3 is the opening of Paul's
second epistle to that troubled church. He says, "Blessed
be the God and Father of our Lord Jesus Christ. In
Romans 15:6, Paul tells of the church's glorifying "the
God and Father of our Lord Jesus Christ."

Other New Testament writers besides Paul wrote from
the same perspective. Peter wrote, "Blessed be the God
and Father of our Lord Jesus Christ" (1 Peter 1:3). The
apostle John wrote in 2 John 3, "Grace, mercy and peace
will be with us, from God the Father and from Jesus
Christ, the Son of the Father."

THERE IS ONLY ONE GOD

Those who say they worship God, and affirm that God
is the eternal living spirit everywhere present, and call
Him Father, but deny that Jesus Christ is essentially the
same as God are offering unacceptable worship. God can
never be worshiped unless He is worshiped as the Father
of the Lord Jesus Christ.

There are those who assert that Moslems, Jews, and
Christians all worship the same God, only in different
ways. That is not true. Our God is the Father of the Lord
Jesus Christ. He cannot be defined in any other terms.
Cultists, so-called Jehovah's Witnesses, or liberals who
claim to worship God yet deny the deity of Jesus Christ
worship a different god from the God of the Bible. They
are offering unacceptable worship.

It is not enough to assert that God is the Father of all

mankind and worship Him on that basis, with no regard
to the biblical understanding of who He is. In the same
context in which He said, "He who has seen Me has seen
the Father," Jesus said, "No one comes to the Father but
through Me" (John 14:6). The only way anyone can ever
come to God is acknowledging Him as the One who is the
Father of our Lord Jesus Christ.

## TRINITARIAN WORSHIP

Trinitarian doctrine, then, is essential to true worship.
John 5:23 is the logical conclusion to Jesus' teaching
that God was uniquely His Father: "That all may honor
the Son, even as they honor the Father. He who does not
honor the Son does not honor the Father who sent Him."
*Honor* is a word that implies worship. We're not only to
worship the Father; we're to worship the Son as well.

That has important implications in terms of the way
we direct our worship. In fact, the only way to worship
the Father is to worship the Son. Thomas fell on his
knees before the resurrected Jesus and said, "My Lord
and my God!" (John 20:28). He was fulfilling the proper
perspective of worship. God can be worshiped only as He
is perceived to be one with His Son, who is to receive the
same honor as the Father.

Jesus urged the Samaritan woman to acknowledge
Him as the Son of God—to worship Him. He didn't have
to say, "Worship Me." He simply affirmed that God is His
Father. And yet the conclusion is the same: Jesus Christ
is Lord. This, then, is the bottom line in all worship: we
come to God only through Christ, and we come to Christ
in coming to God. Worship of the Father cannot be separated from worship of the Son.

We worship the Father, and we worship the Son, but
what about the Holy Spirit? Nothing in Scripture directly
tells us to worship the Holy Spirit, but worship cannot be
separated from His work. It is the Spirit who gives us the
confidence to come into God's presence and cry, "Abba,
Father," according to Galatians 4:6 and Romans 8:15-
16. It is in the Spirit's power and presence that we have
access to worship God.

We know that the Spirit is equal to the Son and the Father, so it seems obvious that He's worthy to be worshiped also. Although, because of its emphasis on the Spirit's ministry, Scripture does not point that out to us specifically, it is a necessary observation. The Holy Spirit is called the Spirit of God in many passages of Scripture. In Romans 8 He is called the Spirit of Christ. He is the radiation of God the Father, the radiation of God the Son, and worthy of worship as such.

Within the Trinity, each member has a unique ministry. The Holy Spirit calls us to the Son, and the Son calls us to the Father. And so in a sense our worship involves all members of the Trinity, and all are worthy to be worshiped.

### THE FOUNDATION OF TRUE WORSHIP

Thus it is apparent that in John 4 when Jesus uses the term *Father*, He is carefully identifying the object of true worship. It is God—not some vague, undefined, spirit being who accepts worship under a number of names and identities, but the God who is the Father of the Lord Jesus Christ and one in essence with Him. And we come to the Father only through the Son and only in the power of the Holy Spirit.

That confirms again that only a genuine believer in Jesus Christ is capable of true worship. Only a Christian has access to the Son through the Spirit, so only a Christian can come before God to offer worship. Remember, Jesus said, "No one comes to the Father but through Me" (John 14:6). The clear word that comes out of John 4 is that God seeks true worshipers—those who will worship Him in a manner acceptable to Him.

# 11

# Worship in Spirit and in Truth

The woman at the well was looking for the proper method of worship, but she saw only two options—the Samaritan method and the Jewish method. Jesus set her up for the divine method by informing her that both ways of worship were unacceptable.

The Samaritan style of worship was done in ignorance. The Samaritans' spiritual knowledge was limited because they rejected all of the Old Testament except the Pentateuch. Their religion was characterized by enthusiastic worship without proper information. They worshiped in spirit, but not in truth. That is why Jesus said, "You worship that which you do not know" (v. 22).

The Jews had the opposite situation. They accepted all the books of the Old Testament. They had the truth but lacked the spirit. When the Pharisees prayed or gave alms or fasted, their hearts weren't in it. Jesus called them hypocrites, phonies, and whitewashed tombs, full of dead men's bones. In Mark 7:6, Jesus told the Pharisees and scribes, "Rightly did Isaiah prophesy of you hypocrites, as it is written, 'This people honors Me with their lips, but their heart is far away from Me.' "

The worship that occurred on Mount Gerizim was

enthusiastic heresy. The worship offered at Jerusalem was barren, lifeless orthodoxy. Jerusalem had the truth but not the spirit. Gerizim had the spirit but not the truth. Jesus rebuked both styles of worship when He said, "God is spirit, and those who worship Him must worship in spirit and in truth" (v. 24).

The two enemies of true worship are Gerizim and Jerusalem. Sincerity, enthusiasm, and aggressiveness are important, but they must be based on truth. And truth is foundational, but if it doesn't result in an eager, excited, enthusiastic heart, it is deficient. Enthusiastic heresy is heat without light. Barren orthodoxy is light without heat.

The same two extremes are still with us today. On the one hand there are groups who get together and hold hands and sway back and forth and sing songs and speak in ecstatic languages. You can't fault their enthusiasm, but it is often zeal without knowledge.

Worshiping with enthusiasm is not enough. No group of worshipers is more spirited than the fanatic Shiite Muslims who once a year slit their scalps with razors and then beat themselves in the head with the flat side of their swords to stimulate bleeding. Men, boys, and even infants have their shaved heads lacerated with swift chopping strokes of a straight razor and then march around in the square before the mosque, bleeding profusely while thousands watch and chant. They do it to celebrate the death of a Muslim leader more than a dozen centuries ago, and they see their hideous display as worship. It stands as an extreme example of what attempting to worship apart from the truth can become.

On the other hand, there are those who hold firmly to sound doctrine but have lost their spirit of enthusiasm. They know the truth but can't get excited about it. Maybe some of them go to your church.

The Father seeks both enthusiasm and orthodoxy, spirit and truth.

WORSHIP IN SPIRIT

What does it mean to worship in spirit? The word *spirit*

in verse 24 refers to the human spirit, the inner person. Worship is to flow from the inside out. It is not a matter of being in the right place, at the right time, with the right words, the right demeanor, the right clothes, the right formalities, the right music, and the right mood. Worship is not an external activity for which an environment must be created. It takes place on the inside, in the spirit.

Paul understood that kind of worship. In Romans 1:9 Paul wrote, "God, whom I serve with my spirit in the preaching of the gospel of His Son, is my witness as to how unceasingly I make mention of you." In the Greek text, the word for "serve" is *latreuo*, that word for worship again. Paul worshiped God in his spirit.

David also worshiped God in his spirit. Psalm 45:1 is the expression of David's worshiping heart: "My heart overflows with a good theme." Psalm 103 says, "Bless the Lord, O my soul; and all that is within me, bless His holy name." That refers to worship that has its origin from within, in the spirit. In Psalm 51, David comes to God in repentance, and he says in verse 15,

O Lord, open my lips,
That my mouth may declare Thy praise.
For Thou dost not delight in sacrifice, otherwise I
    would give it;
Thou art not pleased with burnt offering.
The sacrifices of God are a broken spirit;
A broken and a contrite heart, O God, Thou wilt not
    despise.

David knew that God's primary concern was not the externals, and in his prayer of repentance he appealed to God on that basis. The proof of the reality of his repentance was his broken and contrite heart, not the burnt offerings he gave. And thus it is with all worship. Its genuineness is evidenced in the heart, where true worship originates. His words describe a man whose heart is so filled with praise that all he needs is to get his mouth open so it will come out.

One of the great experiences of my brief life has been to

read *The Existence and Attributes of God,* by Stephen Charnock. Charnock wrote,

> Without the heart it is no worship; it is a stage play; an acting a part without being that person really which is acted by us: a hypocrite, in the notion of the word, is a stage-player. . . . We may be truly said to worship God, though we [lack] perfection; but we cannot be said to worship him, if we [lack] sincerity.[1]

That's very true. We may worship imperfectly but we cannot worship insincerely. As we come to worship God it must be from the depth of what is within us.

HOW TO HAVE A WORSHIPING SPIRIT

On the twenty-sixth Lord's day of 1881 Andrew Bonar wrote in his diary, "During the whole day and every service I felt myself strengthened and upheld by the Lord's presence in Spirit, more than usual. There were moments of great nearness."

That is a description of worship in the spirit, in which there is an overwhelming sense of the nearness of God. James 4:8 says, "Draw near to God and He will draw near to you." I am sure many Christians have rarely experienced that.

We can have overflowing hearts that worship in spirit. First of all *we must be yielded to the Holy Spirit.* Before we can worship God in our spirit, the Holy Spirit has to be there to produce true worship. First Corinthians 2:11 says, "The thoughts of God no one knows except the Spirit of God." If you don't have the Spirit of God prompting your heart, motivating your heart, cleansing your heart, instructing your heart, you cannot worship God, because you cannot even know Him.

"No one can say, 'Jesus is Lord,' except by the Holy Spirit" (1 Corinthians 12:3). In other words, without the Holy Spirit, a person cannot truly affirm the lordship of Christ. To worship Christ as sovereign requires prodding

1. Stephen Charnock, *Discourses upon the Existence and Attributes of God* (New York: Ketcham, n.d.), pp. 225-26.

by the Holy Spirit. And we receive the Holy Spirit only upon the reception of Jesus Christ as Savior and Lord.

Again, that confirms that the foundation of true worship is salvation. One who is not saved cannot truly worship. And one who is truly saved will be motivated by the indwelling Holy Spirit to worship. It is fair, then, to examine ourselves on the basis of our worship. If you have trouble worshiping, maybe you're not saved. If you get bored in church, or if you don't mind missing church altogether, it may be because the Holy Spirit isn't in you prompting your heart. If He is there, we must yield our will to His power.

Second, if we are to worship in spirit, *our thoughts must be centered on God.* Worship is the overflow of a mind renewed by God's truth. We call the process meditation. There seems to be a lot of confusion about what meditation is. Meditation is just focusing the whole mind on one subject, concentrating reason, imagination, and emotion on one reality.

If you find that hard, you are fairly normal. Because of our exposure to television, radio, and other mass media, we have more to think about than any previous civilization. Consequently, our attention span on one theme can be very limited, and we have difficulty focusing long on one subject. Meditation is a discipline we have to train ourselves for.

The heart of meditation is discovery—the discovery of insights from God's truth. And discovery comes out of time spent with God in prayer and in His Word. His Spirit teaches us truth from the Word as we study and meditate on it prayerfully.

Charles Haddon Spurgeon asked, "Why is it that some people are often in a place of worship and yet they're not holy? It is because they neglect their closets. They love the wheat but they do not grind it; they would have the corn but they will not go forth into the field to gather it; the fruit hangs on the tree but they will not pluck it; and the water flows at their feet but they'll not stoop to drink it."

To worship in spirit, then, *we must have an undivided*

*heart.* Without a united heart, worship is impossible. A person with a divided heart may have good intentions, but he finds that when he sits down to pray and spend time with the Lord, a million other things flood his mind. Most of us know that experience.

David was a king. He had more than a few things to worry about. And yet he sought to worship God with an undivided heart. In Psalm 86:11 David prayed, "Unite my heart to fear Thy name." (The expression "fear Thy name" is equivalent to the word *worship.*)

In Psalm 57:7, David wrote, "My heart is steadfast, O God, my heart is steadfast; I will sing, yes, I will sing praises." In other words, the music of praise rises out of a steadfast heart. In Psalm 108 we find the same thought. Verse 1 says, "My heart is steadfast, O God; I will sing, I will sing praises, even with my soul." Worship comes from a steadfast heart, a resolute heart, a determined heart, a heart focused solely on God.

Finally, *we must be repentant.* All sin must be dealt with. When we talk about worship we must talk about cleansing, purging, purifying, confessing, repenting— because the only person who can enter into communion with an utterly holy God is one whose sin is dealt with. We cannot go rushing into God's presence in our impurity, thinking that all is well. We, like Isaiah, must confess before God our sin and allow God to touch that living, burning coal to our lips to purge us.

Often, we know of sin in our lives that needs to be confessed. Other times we may think we are all right in the sight of God but are not. In Psalm 139:23-24, David wrote, "Search me, O God, and know my heart; try me and know my anxious thoughts; and see if there be any hurtful way in me, and lead me in the everlasting way." That is an admission that even David couldn't fully understand his own heart.

Maybe the reason we have difficulty really abandoning ourselves in worship to God, the reason we do not experience the nearness of God, is that we have areas of our lives that are not pure in the sight of God. We all have blind spots and deficiencies only God knows. We must be open, willing to ask God to turn on the searchlight and expose whatever is in the shadows. We must yield our spirits to the Holy Spirit who fills us with His presence and power. We ask Him to cleanse out every corner of our lives—and then the flow of worship can occur.

### THE MAIN HINDRANCE

There is only one hindrance to worshiping in spirit—self. It can come in all kinds of packages, but the result is the same: when we set ourselves in front of God, we cannot worship Him properly. We can blame it on a lack of time, or too many distractions—but we find the time to do the projects and activities we genuinely want to do. The real problem with the one who uses those excuses is that he is too selfish—too lazy and too self-indulgent—to align his priorities properly.

Stephen Charnock wrote,

> To pretend a homage to God, and intend only the advantage of self, is rather to mock him than worship him. When we believe that we ought to be satisfied, rather than God glorified, we set God below ourselves, imagine that he should submit his own honor to our advantage; we make ourselves more glorious than God.[2]

That's the hindrance to worshiping in spirit—to set oneself, one's needs, one's advantages, and one's blessings, above God.

No one can worship in spirit until he dies to the flesh. Jesus described it as denying self. We must set self aside—die to self—and be lost in worshiping God. Then we will know what it is to worship in spirit.

### WORSHIP IN TRUTH

Jesus said we are to worship in truth as well, and thus He linked worship inseparably to truth. Worship is not an emotional exercise with God-words that induce certain feelings. Worship is a response built upon truth.

2. Ibid., p. 241.

Psalm 145:18 says, "The Lord is near to all who call upon Him, to all *who call upon Him in truth*" (emphasis added). Clearly, truth is prerequisite to acceptable worship.

In Psalm 86:11, when David prayed for a united heart, he also asked for an increased understanding of the truth: "Teach me Thy way, O Lord; I will walk in Thy truth; unite my heart to fear Thy name."

Pilate asked the very important question, "What is truth?" (John 18:38). And Jesus answered it in John 17:17 when He said: "Thy word is truth." If we are to worship in truth and the Word of God is truth, we must worship out of an understanding of the Word of God.

PREACH THE WORD

That is why expository preaching and the systematic teaching of the Word of God are so important. Some preachers seem to specialize in sermons that are only marginally biblical but that move the congregation and make them laugh and cry with clever stories and anecdotes. They might be interesting, fun, entertaining, exciting, and impressive sermons, but they do not help the people worship God. The purpose of the ministry is not to create an emotional experience. The calling of every preacher is to teach about God, and out of that foundation of knowledge comes worship.

Any young person going into the ministry who is not committed to expository preaching is cheating his own ministry because people must respond to the truth of the Word of God in every dimension of life. The only effective ministry is that which expounds the Word of God.

Unfortunately, many churches—many evangelical churches—spend so much time with promotion and "preliminaries" that one can't find God in the midst of the program. Our worship must be substantive—based on the Word of God. That elevates the preaching of the Word to the utmost importance in worship. Why, some may wonder, is there such an emphasis on preaching in a worship service? Why not have a brief message, or even no message at all, and just sing songs, pray, praise, and

have testimonies? To ask the question is to reveal ignorance about the reason for and the nature of the pastor-
teacher's task.

The challenge of the pulpit is to bring the people to the
place of worship as a way of life. In *Between Two
Worlds,* John Stott says it well:

> Word and worship belong indissolubly to each other.
> All worship is an intelligent and loving response to the
> revelation of God, because it is the adoration of his
> Name. Therefore acceptable worship is impossible
> without preaching. For preaching is making known the
> Name of the Lord, and worship is praising the Name of
> the Lord made known. Far from being an alien intru-
> sion into worship, the reading and preaching of the
> word are actually indispensable to it. The two cannot
> be divorced. Indeed, it is their unnatural divorce which
> accounts for the low level of so much contemporary
> worship. Our worship is poor because our knowledge
> of God is poor, and our knowledge of God is poor
> because our preaching is poor. But when the Word of
> God is expounded in its fullness, and the congregation
> begin to glimpse the glory of the living God, they bow
> down in solemn awe and joyful wonder before His
> throne. It is preaching which accomplishes this, the
> proclamation of the Word of God in the power of the
> Spirit of God. That is why preaching is unique and irre-
> placeable.[3]

The exposition of the Word, then, is essential to meaningful worship in the assembly of saints. And the insight
gained into God's Word in the worship service will both
deepen the quality of individual worship throughout the
week and stimulate the saints' desire to study the Scriptures daily.

When the early church met together, they met to be
taught the apostles' doctrine—the revelation of God

3. John R. W. Stott, *Between Two Worlds* (Grand Rapids:
   Eerdmans, 1982), pp. 82-83.

about Himself, made manifest through the apostles' writings and teachings. That is why Paul wrote to Timothy,

Be a good servant of Christ Jesus, constantly nourished on the words of the faith and of the sound doctrine which you have been following. But have nothing to do with worldly fables fit only for old women .... Until I come, give attention to the public reading of Scripture, to exhortation and teaching. [1 Timothy 4:6-7, 13]

The Corinthian church had gone to the extreme of enthusiastic, mindless activity. They liked to speak in ecstatic languages and have showy demonstrations that were remnants of their pagan background. They were setting content and truth aside for the sake of external, unintelligible, emotional experiences. Paul rebukes them in 1 Corinthians 14:

For if I pray in a tongue, my spirit prays, but my mind is unfruitful. What is the outcome then? I shall pray with the spirit and I shall pray with the mind also; I shall sing with the spirit and I shall sing with the mind also. Otherwise if you bless in the spirit only, how will the one who fills the place of the ungifted say the "Amen" at your giving of thanks, since he does not know what you are saying? [vv. 14-16]

If therefore the whole church should assemble together and all speak in tongues, and ungifted men or unbelievers enter, will they not say that you are mad? But if all prophecy [speaking forth the Word of God in an understandable language], and an unbeliever or an ungifted man enters, he is convicted by all, he is called to account by all; the secrets of his heart are disclosed; and so he will fall on his face and worship God, declaring that God is certainly among you. [vv. 23-25]

You see, the effect of purely emotional activity is that people get a good feeling. The effect of the truth is that they worship God. Truth is at the heart of worship, and unless enthusiasm and emotion are inseparably linked to the truth, they are meaningless.

Nehemiah 8 shows the power of God's Word to motivate true worship in those whose hearts are open. After Nehemiah and the people had completed the building of the wall of Jerusalem, they asked Ezra to read the scroll that contained the Word of God. Ezra opened the scroll in sight of all the people, and immediately all the people stood up at the presentation of God's Word. "Then Ezra blessed the Lord the great God. And all the people answered, 'Amen, Amen!' while lifting up their hands; then they bowed low and worshiped the Lord with their faces to the ground." The truth of the Scriptures threw them to their faces in an act of worship.

### Where Spirit and Truth Meet

All genuine worship is exactly that kind of heartfelt response to the truth of God and His Word. Truth is the objective factor in worship, and spirit is the subjective. Both must come together.

When the Word of God dominates your life, your praise is regulated, and your worship is conformed to the divine standard. That is why Paul admonished the Colossians, "Let the word of Christ richly dwell within you, with all wisdom teaching and admonishing one another with psalms and hymns and spiritual songs, singing with thankfulness in your hearts to God" (Colossians 3:16). This is the perfect blend: emotion regulated by understanding, enthusiasm directed by the Word of God.

Psalm 47:7 says, "Sing ye praises with understanding" (KJV). Worship is not simply an ecstatic experience, having no meaning or content. Worship is not a good feeling apart from any comprehension of truth. Worship is an expression of praise from the heart, toward a God who is understood as He is truly revealed.

The nature of worship, then, is to offer God worship from the depths of our inner beings in praise, prayer, song, giving, and living, always based upon His revealed truth. The person who would worship God must therefore have a faithful commitment to the Word of God. Worship does not happen by a zap out of heaven that makes us fall down. It is the overflow of our understanding of God as He has revealed Himself in the Scriptures. That is worshiping in spirit and in truth.

# 12

# Glory to God in the Highest

We began chapter 2 with this definition: worship is honor and adoration directed to God. Throughout this study, the concept has expanded, so that perhaps a fuller definition is appropriate: worship is our innermost being responding with praise for all that God is, through our attitudes, actions, thoughts, and words, based on the truth of God as He has revealed Himself.

Another way to say it is that worship is glorifying God. To be wholly obsessed with the glory of God is the consuming passion of the true worshiper, who lives to exalt God. This chapter and the next will be devoted to exploring that truth.

The first question and answer in *The Shorter Catechism* are: "What is the chief end of man? Man's chief end is to glorify God, and to enjoy Him forever." According to the catechism, then, the pinnacle of being is in giving God glory and enjoying Him. The supreme fullness of any individual's purpose is to be totally absorbed in the person of God, and to view all of life through eyes that are filled with the wonder and glory of God's attributes. That is the perspective of the true worshiper.

## WHAT IS GOD'S GLORY?

The word *glory* means "something that is worthy of praise or exaltation; brilliance; beauty; renown." It has been employed to describe everything from football teams with winning histories to sunsets.

God's glory has two aspects. First is His inherent, or *intrinsic glory.* God is the only being in all of existence who can be said to possess inherent glory. We don't give it to Him; it is His by virtue of who He is. If no one ever gave God any praise, He would still be the glorious God that He is, because He was glorious before any beings were created to worship Him.

Men do not have intrinsic glory. Man's glory is granted to him. If you take off a king's robe and crown and put him next to a beggar who has had a bath, you will never know which is which. The glory of the king is external, acquired glory.

God's glory is inherent; it cannot be taken away, it cannot be added to. It is total glory that cannot be diminished. His glory is His being—simply the sum of what He is, regardless of what we do or do not do in recognition of it.

In Exodus 33, Moses, who burned with the desire to know God, said to Him, "I pray Thee, show me Thy glory" (v. 18). God answered, "I Myself will make all My goodness pass before you, and will proclaim the name of the Lord before you" (v. 19). *The name of the Lord* is an often-used biblical phrase that means all that He is—the sum of His attributes. And that is synonymous with God's glory. When He declares His Name, He declares His glory, for His glory is the composite of His attributes.

In Acts 7:2, God is called "the God of glory." Glory is as essential to God as light is to the sun, as blue is to the sky, as wet is to water. You don't make water wet; it is wet. You don't make the sky blue or the sun light; they are those things. You can't take them away. You can't add to them.

God does not give His glory away or share it in any sense. In Isaiah 48:11 God says, "My glory will I not give to another." He will give us temporal blessing, wisdom, riches, and honor, but never His glory. God cannot divest Himself of who He is. He plants His glory within believers, but never apart from Himself. The glory does not become ours—it is still His glory radiating through us—there because God Himself dwells there in the person of the Holy Spirit.

A second aspect to God's glory is *ascribed glory.* That is what the Bible refers to when it speaks of giving God glory. Psalm 29:1-2 says, "Give unto the Lord, O ye mighty, give unto the Lord glory and strength. Give unto the Lord the glory due unto his name; worship the Lord in the beauty of holiness" (KJV).

Obviously, we cannot give God glory in the sense of adding to His glory, any more than we can give Him strength. Yet Psalm 29:2 says, "Give unto the Lord glory and strength." The psalmist is urging us to *recognize* God's glory and acknowledge it.

Although we cannot add to God's glory, we can confirm it and praise Him for it, and we can add to the world's perception of it. Titus 2:9-10 says,

Urge bondslaves to be subject to their masters in everything, to be well-pleasing, not argumentative, not pilfering, but showing all good faith that they may *adorn the doctrine of God* in every respect. [emphasis added]

Of course, that does not mean that we can adorn God. But we can adorn the doctrine of God, by enhancing the teaching of God in the world through godly behavior. A person can live any life he wants, and it won't affect God's nature or alter God's intrinsic glory. What it *will* affect is the testimony about God in the world.

Ascribing glory to God, then, means acknowledging and magnifying His glory. For example, in Philippians 1:20, Paul wrote that his desire was that "as always, so now also Christ shall be magnified in my body." He did not mean that Christ needed to be improved on. He meant that men's view of Christ could be enhanced through him.

Creation itself magnifies God. Psalm 19:1 says, "The

heavens are telling of the glory of God." In other words, God's glory is visible at least in part through creation. Romans 1:20 says, "For since the creation of the world His invisible attributes, His eternal power and divine nature, have been clearly seen, being understood through what has been made." That is exactly what we are to do in ascribing God glory—make His attributes clearly seen to men.

1 Chronicles 16 is a wonderful passage about the glory of God:

> Sing to the Lord, all the earth;
> Proclaim good tidings of His salvation from day to
>     day.
> Tell of His glory among the nations.
> His wonderful deeds among all the peoples.
> For great is the Lord, and greatly to be praised;
> He also is to be feared above all gods.
> For all the gods of the peoples are idols.
> But the Lord made the heavens.
> Splendor and majesty are before Him,
> Strength and joy are in His place.
> Ascribe to the Lord, O families of the peoples,
> Ascribe to the Lord glory and strength
> Ascribe to the Lord the glory due His name.
>
> vv. 23-29

That visible, audible, or otherwise public testimony is what it means to give God glory. It is exalting Him, affirming His attributes, reflecting His character, praising Him for who He is, and making Him known in His fullness.

## WHY SHOULD WE GIVE GOD GLORY?

Why should we glorify God? First, *because He made us.* Psalm 100 says, "It is He who has made us, and not we ourselves." We tend to forget that, thinking that our accomplishments make *us* worthy of praise. But Romans 11:36 says, "For from Him and through Him and to Him are all things. To Him be the glory forever, Amen." As Creator, He alone is worthy to be glorified.

The apostle John describes an incident in heaven when the twenty-four elders cast their crowns before the throne of God and said, "Worthy art Thou, our Lord and our God, to receive glory and honor and power; for Thou didst create all things, and because of Thy will they existed, and were created" (Revelation 4:11). God gave us our being, our life, and everything that is. How could we give glory to any other, or take it for ourselves? We are what we are because God made us.

Second, we ought to glorify God *because God made everything to give Him glory.* The whole purpose of creation is to glorify God. Proverbs 16:4 says, "The Lord hath made all things for himself" (KJV). Everything in creation is designed to radiate His attributes—His power, His love, His mercy, His wisdom, His grace. That is not egotism on God's part. He *is* worthy of our praise. As God, He has every right to demand worship and adoration from His creatures.

Inevitably, He will be glorified by everyone. Ultimately all men give God glory, willingly or unwillingly, in life or in death. The glory God gets from the righteous is what especially pleases Him. They give Him glory willingly. In fact, giving Him glory is the special calling of God's people. In Isaiah 43:21, God says, "The people whom I formed for Myself, will declare My praise." First Peter 2:9 says of the church, "You are a chosen race, a royal priesthood, a holy nation, a people for God's own possession, that you may proclaim the excellencies of Him who has called you."

Unbelieving men may not want to give God glory, but they will. Pharaoh was determined not to glorify God, but (Exodus 14:17) God said, "I will be honored through Pharaoh and all his army, through his chariots and his horsemen." And He was. God's message to Pharaoh was, "Indeed, for this cause I have allowed you to remain, in order to show you My power, and in order to proclaim My name through all the earth" (Exodus 9:16). That is exactly what happened. Although Pharaoh would not glorify God with his life, God was glorified in his destruction.

That is itself another incentive for giving God glory. We

should want to give Him glory *because He judges those who don't.* According to Romans 1, lost men are condemned because they refuse and corrupt God's glory: "Because that, when they knew God, they glorified him not as God ... and changed the glory of the uncorruptible God into an image made like unto corruptible man" (vv. 21-23, KJV). The theme of Romans 1 with regard to God's dealings with those who refuse His glory is found in the words *God gave them up* (see vv. 24, 26, 28). God simply abandoned them to their depravity. He is glorified and revealed as a holy, righteous God in judging them.

Jeremiah 13 records a message the prophet Jeremiah gave to Israel. His ministry was a frustrating one; the people did not listen to anything he said until they were about to be taken into captivity. His heart was grieved, as he cried out,

> Listen and give heed, do not be haughty,
> For the Lord hath spoken.
> Give glory to the Lord your God.
> Before He brings darkness
> And before your feet stumble
> On the dusky mountains,
> And while you are hoping for light
> He makes it into deep darkness,
> And turns it to gloom.

vv. 15-16

In other words, you ought to give God glory because if you don't, you are going to be judged.

In chapter 3 we looked at the account of the angel described in Revelation 14:6-7 who is said to possess the eternal gospel. His message was, "Fear God, and give Him glory, *because the hour of His judgment has come*" (emphasis added). Again God's glorious judgment is certain for those who refuse to worship Him and give Him glory.

WORSHIP AND GOD'S GLORY

Those who give God glory willingly are true worshipers, and worship is nothing more, nothing less than glorifying God with a joyful, willing heart. Whatever can be said, then, about how to glorify God, is further insight into the subject of genuine worship.

Glorifying God begins, as we have clearly seen, with salvation, when we submit to Jesus Christ as Lord, thereby becoming true worshipers. Philippians 2:9-10 says of the Lord Jesus, "God highly exalted Him, and bestowed on Him the name which is above every name, that at the name of Jesus every knee should bow, of those who are in heaven, and on earth, and under the earth, *and that every tongue should confess that Jesus Christ is Lord, to the glory of God the Father"* (emphasis added).

And as worship is a way of life, so glorifying God must be the worshiper's conscious, continual, purposeful, and perpetual aim. First Corinthians 10:31, a well-known but too-little practiced verse, gives the strategy of a true worshiper's life: "Whether, then, you eat or drink or whatever you do, do all to the glory of God." Whatever we do, beginning with activities as mundane as eating and drinking, ought to be done to His glory.

Jesus spoke of the evil of the days of Noah: "For as in those days which were before the flood they were eating and drinking, they were marrying and giving in marriage, until the day that Noah entered the ark, and they did not understand until the flood came and took them all away" (Matthew 24:38-39). Jesus was not condemning them for eating and drinking per se. There is nothing inherently evil in those activities—they are normal, necessary functions of life. The error was in doing those things with no thought of glorifying God. They didn't understand until the Flood came and washed them away that we are on this earth for God's glory alone, and every activity of life must be directed to that purpose.

That is how Jesus lived. He said, "I do not seek My own glory" (John 8:50). "He who is seeking the glory of the one who sent Him, He is true, and there is no unrighteousness in Him" (John 7:18). Jesus' life purpose was to bring God glory, to radiate His attributes, to adorn the doctrine of God—even if that meant obedience unto death. And in living that kind of life, He established the pattern for every true worshiper (see 1 Peter 2:21).

Living for God's glory eliminates the possibility of hypocrisy. A hypocrite is one who deliberately tries to steal glory from God. He wants a little glory for himself. Jesus indicts the hypocrites in Matthew 6:1:

> Beware of practicing your righteousness before men to be noticed by them; otherwise, you have no reward with your Father who is in heaven. When therefore you give alms, do not sound a trumpet before you, as the hypocrites do in the synagogues and in the streets, that they may be honored by men.

When we purpose to devote our lives to God's glory, we cannot possibly seek our own glory. Whatever you do in the Lord's work—whether you teach a Bible class, witness, pray, give money, rebuke sin, or any other good work—if your motive is to impress men or get personal adulation, God cannot truly bless your efforts. If we try to steal a little glory for ourselves, we have stolen the blessing and joy that comes from God.

A student once thought he would impress D. L. Moody. The young man had been in an all-night prayer meeting and was feeling especially spiritual. He came to Mr. Moody and said, "Do you know where we've been? We've been at an all-night prayer meeting. See how our faces shine?"

Mr. Moody, unimpressed, quoted Exodus 34:29: "Moses knew not that his face shone."

Devoting our lives to God's glory means sacrificing self. It means that we prefer God above all else. The true worshiper does not think about how much it's going to help him, how much money he is going to get, how much success he will realize, how much fame he will have, how many friends he can garner, how spiritual he may appear to others, and so on. The pursuit of the glory of God is a purely selfless, lonely pursuit. True worship is not concerned with the popularity of the stand it takes, or the kind of response it gets.

## PAYING THE PRICE

To seek to glorify God above all else can be costly. Exodus 32 is the account of some people who paid a very dear price for God's glory. When Moses came down from the mountain after receiving the law from God, he found the people of Israel worshiping a golden calf. They were stealing God's glory right at the foot of Mount Sinai. They were having an orgy, and Aaron was leading it.

Moses was furious. He stood at the gate of the camp and said, "Whoever is for the Lord, come to me!" (v. 26). All the sons of Levi—the priests—came. Verse 27 says, "And he said to them, 'Thus says the Lord, the God of Israel, "Every man of you put his sword upon his thigh, and go back and forth from gate to gate in the camp, and kill every man his brother, and every man his friend, and every man his neighbor." ' "

The glory of God was at stake, and those who wanted to defend it were called upon to perform a difficult task. They had to kill people they loved, for the sake of the glory of God. God wanted to show the world for all time that He would share His glory with no one. "About three thousand men of the people fell that day" (v. 28). It was a high price to pay for the glory of God.

God will not call us to kill our loved ones for His glory, but He may ask us to forsake them, and He will often call us to take unpopular stands on important issues. He will require us to pay a price to glorify Him. And the one who truly wants to glorify God will be content to do His will at any cost.

Jesus said to Peter, "When you were younger, you used to gird yourself, and walk wherever you wished; but when you grow old, you will stretch out your hands [meaning that he would be crucified], and someone else will gird you, and bring you where you do not wish to go. Now this He said, signifying by what kind of death he would glorify God" (John 21:18-19). In other words, Peter paid the price of death by crucifixion to glorify God.

Peter wrote his first epistle to encourage suffering believers with the truth that their suffering was unto

God's glory. He wrote, "To the degree that you share the sufferings of Christ, keep on rejoicing; so that also at the revelation of His glory, you may rejoice with exultation" (1 Peter 4:14). Paul underscored that when he wrote, "For I consider that the sufferings of this present time are not worthy to be compared with the glory that is to be revealed to us" (Romans 8:18).

Living for God's glory always involves suffering, and there is more than one kind of suffering. Everyone is sensitive to his own hurts, and as believers we take great comfort in the fact that Jesus suffers when we suffer. But the mature Christian, the committed worshiper, has a different perspective. He suffers greatest when God suffers. That is, he suffers when God's name is slandered or when His glory is not acknowledged. Rather than rejoicing that God identifies with his suffering, he rejoices in the privilege of sharing God's suffering.

Psalm 69:9 makes this powerful statement: "For zeal for Thy house has consumed me. And the reproaches of them who reproach Thee have fallen on me." David penned those words, but they had a Messianic import, and Jesus quoted them as applying to Himself when He purged the Temple. That verse describes one so caught up with the glory of God that He takes every blasphemy, every insult to God, as a personal blow.

That is the mind-set of the true worshiper, the one who has committed his life to the glory of God. He is consumed with zeal—not for his own reputation or self-image, but for the glory and majesty of almighty God, to whom he has devoted his whole being to worship. That is the only kind of life acceptable to God.

# 13

# How to Glorify God

Worship is not mystical, it is intensely practical. Glorifying God is nothing if it is not active and dynamic. One of the great tragedies of contemporary Christianity is that we have allowed the concept of worship to degenerate to the point that many people think of worship as sitting quietly and piously, dreamily contemplating some abstract and ethereal noumenon.

Such an approach bears no relationship whatever to real worship. Worship is deliberate, purposeful, and active. It involves not just the thought process, but the whole being as well. The life of a true worshiper is a joyous, vibrant life—a life of actively seeking to glorify God in practical ways.

Scripture is specific about the ways we can glorify God. In this chapter I would like to examine several responses to God's glory that may be considered acts of pure, acceptable worship.

CONFESSION OF SIN

We worship God and give Him glory when we confess our sin. First John 1:9 is familiar: "If we confess our sins, He is faithful and just to forgive us our sins and to cleanse us from all unrighteousness." The word "confess" in that verse is *homologeo*, which comes from the union of two Greek words—*homo*, meaning "the same," and *logos*, meaning "expression." It literally means "to express complete agreement." Confession is fully agreeing with God about the responsibility for sin and the awfulness of it.

We don't often think of the confession of sin as worship, but it is. When we confess our sins, we are humbling ourselves before God, acknowledging His holiness, experiencing His faithfulness and righteousness in forgiving us, accepting any chastisement He may give, and therefore glorifying Him.

In fact, confession serves the dual purpose of being an act of worship itself and of preparing the repentant sinner to worship. Hebrews 9:14 says cleansing purifies the conscience "to serve the living God." The Greek word for *serve* in that verse again is *latreuo*, which means "worship." The purifying that takes place in confession and forgiveness is an important preparation to worship.

The Old Testament account of Achan is an example of how God is glorified in confession of sin. Achan disobeyed God by stealing treasure from the city of Jericho. He thought if he buried it in his tent, no one would ever know. But God saw right through the dirt, and He was so displeased with Achan that the entire nation of Israel suffered because of it. They were defeated in battle at Ai, and many Israelites died in a graphic illustration that God cannot bless our sin.

When Joshua realized what had happened and Achan's sin was about to be revealed, He said to Achan, "My son, I implore you, give glory to the Lord, the God of Israel, and give praise to Him; and tell me now what you have done. Do not hide it from me" (Joshua 7:19). Joshua made the logical connection between the confession of sin and glorifying God.

It is an appropriate parallel. Confessing sin is glorifying God; it exonerates God and acknowledges that He is holy when He acts in judgment against evil. That preserves Him from any accusation of evil in chastening and thus gives Him glory.

Excusing sin, on the other hand, is impugning God. Refusing to acknowledge our responsibility for sin is blaming God.

That is what Adam did. After he sinned, he tried to lay the blame elsewhere: "The woman whom *Thou* gavest to be with me, she gave me from the tree, and I ate" (Genesis 3:12, emphasis added). At first sight it seems like he was blaming the woman, but a closer look shows that he was actually implying that God, who made him and gave him Eve, was ultimately responsible for the situation in which Adam found himself. He was assigning to God the responsibility for unrighteousness, casting aspersions on the character of God.

The apostle John records an interesting statement in his description of the plagues that are to be poured out on the earth during the Tribulation. Revelation 16:8-9 says,

> And the fourth angel poured out his bowl upon the sun; and it was given to it to scorch men with fire. And men were scorched with fierce heat; and they blasphemed the name of God who has power over these plagues; and they did not repent, so as to give Him glory.

To acknowledge their sin and repent would have glorified God, for it would have been an admission that He did what He had to and all His ways were right. They were judged, however, because they refused the worship of confession.

IMPLICIT FAITH IN GOD

God is glorified when we trust Him unquestioningly. Faith is perhaps the basic form of worship. Romans 4:20 says, "[Abraham] did not waver in unbelief, but grew strong in faith, giving glory to God."

Every Christian will *say* that he believes God keeps His Word, but so few Christians live lives of total trust that the world isn't always sure of the trustworthiness of our God. The slightest doubt about God or His goodness or His Word implies that He is not all He says He is. First John 5:10 says, "The one who does not believe God has made Him a liar." In other words, when you doubt God, you make Him appear to be unfaithful.

God's clear promise is, "No temptation has overtaken you but such as is common to man; and God is faithful, who will not allow you to be tempted beyond what you are able, but with the temptation will provide a way of escape also, that you may be able to endure it." If we say that we cannot bear our temptations and the trials of life, we call God a liar.

For some reason, we think of doubt and worry as "small" sins. But when a Christian displays unbelief, care, or an inability to cope with life, he is saying to the world, "My God cannot really be trusted," and that kind of disrespect makes one guilty of a fundamental error, the heinous sin of dishonoring God. That is no small sin.

A good example of unwavering faith is the account of the three young men in the fiery furnace. Daniel 3 tells us that before Nebuchadnezzar cast them into the white-hot furnace he gave them a chance to recant their faith in God and worship a golden image of the king instead. Verse 17 is their answer to Him: "Our God whom we serve is able to deliver us from the furnace of blazing fire; and He will deliver us out of your hand, O king." Then they added, *"But even if He does not,* let it be known to you, O king, that we are not going to serve your gods or worship the golden image that you have set up" (v. 18, emphasis added).

They were in an extremely difficult position. No child of God on record had ever experienced the threat of a fiery furnace, and there were no convenient ready-reference Bible verses they could look to for a promise that they would survive. If they had succumbed to the circumstances, God would not have been glorified. Instead, they took a confident stand of faith in the goodness and justice of God. Their faith was vindicated, and God was glorified in the eyes of an entire nation.

ABUNDANCE OF FRUIT

Fruitful believers also glorify God. In John 15:8, Jesus said, "By this is My Father glorified, that you bear much fruit." Bearing spiritual fruit, then, is an essential part of true worship. A parallel passage is Psalm 92:13-15:

> Planted in the house of the Lord,
> They will flourish in the courts of our God.
> They will still yield fruit in old age;
> They shall be full of sap and very green,
> To declare that the Lord is upright.

Philippians 1:10-11 confirms that spiritual fruit glorifies God. "Approve the things that are more excellent, in order to be sincere and blameless until the day of Christ; having been filled with the fruit of righteousness which comes through Jesus Christ, to the glory and praise of God."

Colossians 1:10 says, "Walk in a manner worthy of the Lord, to please Him in all respects, bearing fruit in every good work." That explains clearly what fruitfulness is. The fruit we bear to His glory is the fruit of good works. Ephesians 5:9 says, "The fruit of light consists in all goodness and righteousness and truth."

Galatians 5 expands that, demonstrating that fruit can manifest itself in attitudes as well as actions: "The fruit of the Spirit is love, joy, peace, patience, kindness, goodness, faithfulness, gentleness, self-control." Fruit, we could say, is anything in our lives that reflects the character of God.

Heine, the German philosopher, said, "You show me your redeemed life and I might believe in your redeemer." Spiritual fruit is evidence to the world of the results of an obedient life. The fruit we bear reveals the character of God to those who don't know Him. Just as literal fruit on a tree is a genetic reproduction of the characteristics of the parent tree, so spiritual fruit is a reproduction of the characteristics of Jesus Christ, who said, "I am the true vine" (John 15:1).

## VERBAL PRAISE

We glorify God, too, by praising Him with our mouths. In Psalm 50:23, God says, "Whoso offereth praise glorifieth me" (KJV). Praise is simply exalting God by reciting His attributes and His works and thanking Him for what He is and what He has accomplished. Many of the psalms are pure expressions of that kind of praise, and Psalm 107 repeatedly uses the refrain "Oh that men would praise the Lord for his goodness, and for his wonderful works to the children of men" (KJV).

The best way to learn to trust God in the present is to study His works from the past. God has already established the pattern of His faithfulness, and His wondrous works are a continual reminder that He has never proved unfaithful. Remembering that and reciting it glorifies Him.

On the day of Pentecost, when believers were first filled with the Holy Spirit and spoke in languages, the message of the words they spoke, translated by God into the languages of their listeners, was "the mighty deeds of God" (Acts 2:11).

Luke 17 tells the story of a group of lepers. Because their disease was so horrible and so contagious, lepers had to separate themselves from society. They were outcasts to be avoided, and everyone stayed as far away as he could. Except Jesus:

> And it came about while He was on the way to Jerusalem, that He was passing between Samaria and Galilee. And as He entered a certain village, ten leprous men who stood at a distance met Him; and they raised their voices, saying, "Jesus, Master, have mercy on us!" And when He saw them, He said to them, "Go and show yourselves to the priests." And it came about that as they were going, they were cleansed. Now one of them, when he saw that he had been healed, turned back, glorifying God with a loud voice, and fell on his face at His feet, giving thanks to Him. And he was a Samaritan. And Jesus answered and said, "Were there not ten cleansed? But the nine—where are they? Was

no one found who turned back to give glory to God, except this foreigner?"

It was a sad, unbelievable situation; of ten lepers saved from a life of sickness and shame, only one thought to glorify God by praising Him for His wonderful work of grace.

## A WILLINGNESS TO SUFFER

We worship God by loving Him enough to suffer for Him. In the previous chapter, we noted that living for the glory of God always involves suffering. You will recall that Peter was called to glorify God by dying for Him. Peter took that challenge to heart, and his life and writings are a study of the relationship of suffering and glory. It is the theme of his first epistle.

He wrote, "If you are reviled for the name of Christ, you are blessed . . . If anyone suffers as a Christian, let him not feel ashamed, but in that name let him glorify God" (1 Peter 4:14-16).

Micaiah was cast in prison. Isaiah was sawn asunder. Paul was beheaded. Tradition says that Luke was hanged on an olive tree and Peter was crucified upside down. Thus did they glorify God. It may be that God will call us to suffer martyrdom, but whether or not He does, we must worship Him by the *willingness* to suffer even death for Him. To suffer for Him is the supreme honor to His holy name. It says you count Him as ultimate.

## A CONTENTED HEART

The true worshiper also lives a life of contentment, regardless of circumstances. Contentment testifies to the wisdom and sovereignty of God and thereby glorifies Him. Discontent, on the other hand, is essentially rebelliousness. The discontented person is, in effect, blaming God.

The message of Philippians 4 is "rejoice in the Lord always; again I say, rejoice!" (v. 4). Beginning in verse 10, we see an illustration of Paul's attitude of complete contentment. The Philippians had sent him a gift of some money, and he wrote to thank them for it:

> I rejoiced in the Lord greatly, that now at last you have revived your concern for me; indeed, you were concerned before, but you lacked opportunity. Not that I speak in respect of want; *for I have learned to be content in whatever circumstances I am.* I know how to get along with humble means, and I also know how to live in prosperity; in any and every circumstance I have learned the secret of being filled and going hungry, both of having abundance and suffering need. I can do all things through Him who strengthens me. [vv. 10-13, emphasis added]

How to have that kind of contentment is a lesson very few people have learned. In verse 17, Paul adds these words: "Not that I seek the gift itself, but I seek for the profit which increases to your account." In other words, Paul was more glad that the Philippians were growing and bearing fruit than he was for the money. He concludes in verses 19-20 by expressing the praise and confidence overflowing in his heart because of his contentment: "And my God shall supply all your needs according to His riches in glory in Christ Jesus. *Now to our God and Father be glory forever and ever. Amen"* (emphasis added).

It is easy to be content when you have received a gift of money, but Paul was content in adverse circumstances as well. When Paul wrote that he could be content in adversity, he was not speaking out of hand—he had been through all kinds of adversity. Second Corinthians 11:23-28 is a catalogue of the things Paul had suffered:

> [I have been] in far more labors, in far more imprisonments, beaten times without number, often in danger of death. Five times I received from the Jews thirty-nine lashes. Three times I was beaten with rods, once I was stoned, three times I was shipwrecked, a night and a day I have spent in the deep. I have been on frequent journeys, in dangers from rivers, dangers from robbers,

dangers from my countrymen, dangers from the Gentiles, dangers in the city, dangers in the wilderness, dangers on the sea, dangers among false brethren; I have been in labor and hardship, through many sleepless nights, in hunger and thirst, often without food, in cold and exposure. Apart from such external things, there is the daily pressure upon me of concern for all the churches.

In addition, he assumed the burdens of other believers: "Who is weak without my being weak? Who is led into sin without my intense concern?" (v.29). Paul wrote, "If I must needs glory, I will glory of the things which concern my infirmities" (v. 30, KJV). He didn't write, "I'll give God glory in spite of my pain." He wrote, "I'll give God glory *because* of it." Such contentment marks true, spiritual worship.

## CONFIDENT PRAYER

Additionally, worship and prayer are inseparable. John 14:13 is a clear statement that prayer glorifies God: "And whatever you ask in My name, that will I do, that the Father may be glorified in the Son."

It does not say that we can ask God for anything and He will give it to us. The prerequisite is that our requests must be in Jesus' name—and that does not mean that we simply tag every prayer with the words, *In Jesus' name. Amen.* Praying in Jesus' name means praying on behalf of Jesus, asking in line with what He desires. Our requests must be in accordance with His will. It is not possible to pray in Jesus' name for something He does not want.

That eliminates selfish requests. It also means that before we pray, we must understand the mind of Christ. Many Christians tend to view prayer only as a way to get things, or as a way to get out of things. We seem to have lost the concept of prayer as communion—living in the consciousness of God's wonderful presence and communing with Him there, learning His thoughts and desires and praying for their fulfillment—"Thy will be done."

The consummation of such praying is when God is glorified in the answer. Prayer does not inform God of things He hasn't heard—its purpose is to allow Him to manifest His glory in giving an answer. The more specific our prayers, the more clearly His glory will be revealed in the answer. And ultimately, His glory is more important than the answer to the prayer.

A CLEAR WITNESS

We worship God by proclaiming His Word with clarity. Paul wrote to the Thessalonians, "Brethren, pray for us that the word of the Lord may spread rapidly and be glorified, just as it did with you" (2 Thessalonians 3:1). When His Word is given exposure, when people hear it and are saved, God is glorified. Acts 13:48-49 records the response to Paul's preaching: "And when the Gentiles heard this, they began rejoicing and glorifying the word of the Lord; and as many as had been appointed to eternal life believed. And the word of the Lord was being spread through the whole region."

God's glory is inherent in His Word, so whenever we give His Word exposure, we are glorifying Him. And when we proclaim the Word and by it bring others to Christ, we are glorifying God in the supreme way, for when a person is redeemed, he too begins to worship in spirit and truth and devotes his life to the glory of God. Worship begets worshipers, and the cycle of glorifying God is begun again in the new believer's life.

Obviously, there are many more ways indicated in Scripture to worship and glorify God, but from what we have examined in these passages that specifically state how God is glorified, it is evident that true worship is an active, all-consuming, never-ending pursuit. As the worshiper gives his life to the glory of God, he discovers a rich resource of joy and power and meaning not available to everyone, for the life that honors God is the only life God honors.

# 14

# Worship as It Was
# Meant to Be

Worship, we have seen, involves all that is inside a person, all that is outside a person, and all that takes place within the corporate assembly of God's people. William Temple, years ago, defined worship this way: "To worship is to quicken the conscience by the holiness of God, to feed the mind with the truth of God, to purge the imagination by the beauty of God, to open the heart to the love of God, and to devote the will to the purpose of God."

Worship is all that we are, reacting rightly to all that He is. In this study we have examined the importance of worship. We have seen that the basis, the foundation, for worship is personal salvation. We have established that its only valid object is the true and living God, as He has revealed Himself in His Word. We have determined that the sphere of worship is everywhere and at all times, and especially in the corporate assembly of the redeemed. We have discussed the essence of worship, and seen that it must be perfectly balanced between spirit and truth—the Word of God and the heart. And we have highlighted a few practical ways to glorify God and worship as were are meant to. Finally, we want to get an overview of acceptable worship and how it affects our lives, and that

will walk us through many of the truths we have already
seen.

## PREPARING TO WORSHIP

Acceptable worship does not happen spontaneously.
Preparation is essential. In a worship service, for example, the choir prepares, the preacher prepares, and the
organist and other musicians prepare. But the most
important preparation of all is the preparation of the
individual worshiper, and that is usually the most
neglected. How does one translate all the truth about
worship we have studied into preparation for worship?

Hebrews 10:22, a call to worship, gives rich insight
into what kind of preparation God expects from a
worshiper:

Let us draw near with a sincere heart in full assurance
of faith, having our hearts sprinkled clean from an evil
conscience and our bodies washed with pure water.

That verse suggests four checkpoints to test our readi-
ness for worship. The first is *sincerity.* We must draw
near "with a true heart." Acceptable worship requires a
heart fixed on God and His glory. Hypocrisy is fatal to
worship. So are double-mindedness, preoccupation with
self, and apathy. We cannot rush into the presence of
God with a heart that is not sincere. That much, at least,
ought to be clear from all that we have learned.

A second checkpoint in preparing to worship is *fidelity:* "Draw near . . . in full assurance of faith." The writer
to the Hebrews was addressing people accustomed to the
Old Covenant, and they were trying to hang on to it. But
the New Covenant had come, with new revelation in
Jesus Christ, and the mysteries of the Old Testament
were unfolding. To worship God the Hebrews had to say
no to the Old Covenant and its ceremonies, sacrifices,
symbols, pictures, and types. The old was gone—it was
set aside. A new and better covenant had come, and they
had to be willing to come to God in full confidence of the
revealed faith of the New Testament.

The New Covenant, in contrast to the old, is not a system based on ceremonies, sacrifices, and external obedience to the law. It requires the worshiper to come to God fully assured that his access is by faith in Jesus Christ. Worshiping in full assurance of faith simply is worshiping according to the truth that faith alone is the ground for acceptance by God. Personal good works, worthiness, self-righteousness, rituals, and other deeds of the flesh do not give us access to God. The true worshiper must come only on the basis of his faith. That is fidelity.

A third checkpoint is *humility*. Hebrews 10:22 says, "Let us draw near . . . having our hearts sprinkled from an evil conscience." While we come to God confidently, in full assurance of faith, we must nevertheless come humbled because of our own unworthiness, knowing we have no right being there without purification by the blood of Jesus Christ, because our hearts are evil.

The final checkpoint in Hebrews 10:22 is *purity*. "Let us draw near . . . having . . . our bodies washed with pure water." That refers not to a literal washing of the body, but rather to the daily confession and spiritual purging necessary to deal with the sins of our humanness. The sprinkling with the blood of Christ that occurs at conversion is a permanent and complete cleansing of the life, but our feet tend to pick up the dust of the world in which we live and walk, and they require a periodic washing.

An incident that occurred the night Jesus was betrayed illustrates the need for such cleansing. Jesus had gone with His disciples to a room where they were to partake of the Passover meal together. In violation of the social customs of the day, no servant was there to wash the feet of the men, dirty from walking the dusty roads. None of the disciples, who were arguing about their greatness in the Kingdom, offered to perform the menial task. Apparently everyone was prepared just to ignore the rather obvious gaffe. Everyone, that is, except Jesus Himself, who, in the role of a servant, took a washbasin and towel and began to wash the feet of the disciples.

When He came to Peter, Peter was going to refuse to let Him do it. "Never shall you wash my feet!" he said (John 13:8). But Jesus answered, "If I do not wash you, you have no part with Me" (v. 8), upon which Peter responded, "Lord, not my feet only, but also my hands and my head" (v. 9). Jesus said to Peter, "He who has bathed needs only to wash his feet, but is completely clean" (v. 10).

First John 1:9 talks about that touch-up cleansing: "If we confess our sins, He is faithful and righteous to forgive us our sins and to cleanse [keep on cleansing] us from all unrighteousness." That daily confession and cleansing from the defilement of sins is a prerequisite to coming into the presence of God, and therefore it is a prerequisite to acceptable worship.

These, then, are the checkpoints: sincerity, fidelity, humility, and purity. Without them we are not prepared to enter God's presence to worship. If, however, we can pass those checkpoints, we may draw near in full confidence, and God will draw near to us. That is the divine promise, and worship reaches its most sublime heights when the worshiper is living in God's presence, in the glow of His glory, a life of worship.

## WORSHIP THAT OVERCOMES THE BARRIERS

Too few Christians, I fear, seem to experience that kind of worship. Many people come to church for years but never really draw nigh unto God, and never clearly have a sense of God's drawing near to them. They complain that worship is difficult, and in their private devotional lives they seem to face insurmountable barriers. Worship as God intends need not be hindered by such barriers, as we see by some of the kinds of barrier-breaking worship that are offered in the Scriptures.

One is *the worship of repentance.* David had sinned a great sin that had certainly resulted in a barrier between himself and God. He had committed adultery with Bathsheba, and then had her husband murdered. Bathsheba had conceived a child as a result of their sin, and the little child born of that union died. David knew that God was punishing him. This was David's response: "David arose from the ground, washed, anointed himself, and changed his clothes; and he came into the house of the Lord and worshiped" (2 Samuel 12:20).

That is the worship of repentance. David was in the midst of a tragic situation—the loss of his infant son— and yet he worshiped God, because he knew he was receiving what he deserved. Even in his chastening he worshiped.

Chastening always calls for praise. God chastens us because He loves us, and our hearts ought to respond with worship. Genuine repentance is when the soul says, "I have sinned and I deserve to be chastised. I have erred against the truth, and more important, I have sinned against God." Right in the midst of chastening, the worship of repentance results in a pouring out of the heart to God, a confession of guilt, and an acknowledgment that we are getting what we deserve, no matter what the calamity. Where there is no praise, where there is anger and bitterness against God, there has been no genuine repentance and confession of sin.

That is how David could enter into the house of the Lord and worship God even while God was smiting him. And that is the kind of commitment to worship God's people need.

A second kind of worship that breaks down barriers is *the worship of submission.* When Job heard the news that everything he loved was gone, his possessions, his animals, and his children, he worshiped the worship of submission. The Bible says, "Job arose and tore his robe and shaved his head, and he fell to the ground, and worshiped" (Job 1:20). Many people would have been bitter and cursed God.

Job had not sinned like David. God was not chastising him for sin—He was allowing Satan to test Job for His own purposes. Yet Job said, "Naked I came from my mother's womb, and naked I shall return there. The Lord gave and the Lord has taken away. Blessed be the name of the Lord." His response was unquestioning submission.

Many people are not able to worship God because they refuse to accept their places in life, their jobs, their careers, their partners, their children, or the other circumstances God brings into life. Their response is bitterness, and they cannot worship.

Job was able to look beyond his present circumstances and see the goodness of God in His plan. Job said: "He knows the way I take; when He has tried me, I shall come forth as gold" (23:10). When God does bring negative circumstances into our lives He always has a positive purpose.

In fact, we invariably get into trouble when we don't have problems because we don't really grow. In Jeremiah 48:11, God is preparing to judge Moab, and He says,

Moab has been at ease since his youth;
He has also been undisturbed on his lees,
Neither has he been emptied from vessel to vessel,
Nor has he gone into exile.
Therefore he retains his flavor, and his aroma has not changed.

The people of Moab had had it so easy and so smooth that they had become rancid. The analogy Jeremiah uses is from winemaking. Winemakers in Jeremiah's day put crushed grapes in a container and let them sit. Eventually the bitterness and the sediment—called the lees, or the dregs—would settle into the bottom. The winemaker would pour the wine off the top into another vessel, and the remaining bitterness would settle into the bottom of the second container in more sediment. Then he would pour that wine into another container, and another, and another—and over a period of time, all of the sediment and its bitterness would be removed (they used it to make vinegar), and the wine would have the aroma of sweetness that the winemaker wanted it to have.

Moab had never lost its bitterness, because the people had never been poured from difficult situation to difficult situation, where the bitterness could be purged out.

We are better off in life if God pours us from trial to trial to trial, because each time we're poured into a different trial, each time we're confined in a different undesirable circumstance, a little of the bitterness of life is removed.

Finally one day God pours us out of the last trial and all that remains is the sweet aroma that He was after all the time—the bitterness is all gone.

A third type, *the worship of devotion*, is seen in the life of Abraham. God had commanded Abraham to offer his son Isaac as an offering to God. That meant slaying him and burning him on an altar. Genesis 22 relates what happened:

> So Abraham rose early in the morning and saddled his donkey, and took two of his young men with him and Isaac his son; and he split wood for the burnt offering, and arose and went to the place of which God had told him. On the third day Abraham raised his eyes and saw the place from a distance. And Abraham said to his young men," "Stay here with the donkey, and I and the lad will go yonder; and we will worship."

It seems incredible that Abraham, knowing that God was going to take the life of his own son, was able to see it as worship. He had devoted himself to worship no matter what the cost. He saw beyond the barriers of pain, difficulty, and the loss of his son, and worshiped. Some people do not worship God because they feel it may cause them a little sacrifice of time and effort. How far is that from being willing to plunge a knife in the chest of your own beloved son—and call it worship, because God commanded it?

It is worthy of note that Abraham did not use the word *sacrifice*. He saw beyond that. He was so devoted to worshiping God that he saw beyond the immediate agony and was willing to pay the awful price if that was what God wanted. Like every true and total worshiper, he was willing to offer the worship of devotion, though it cost the supreme price.

## THE RESULTS OF WORSHIP AS IT WAS MEANT TO BE

When God's people worship as God requires, several results can be observed. First, and obviously, *God is glorified*. Glorifying God, we have seen, is the most crucial element of worship. Worship is ascribing glory to God, recognizing His glory and offering praise to Him for it. God demands it. In Leviticus 10:3, He says, "By those who come near Me, I will be treated as holy, and before all the people I will be honored."

God wants to be set apart and be glorified among His people. Worship accomplishes that. As we said, Psalm 50:23 says, "Whoso offereth praise, glorifieth me" (KJV). And if that were all worship accomplished, it would be enough. But it isn't.

When we worship God as He desires to be worshiped, *believers are purified.* As we saw in chapter 7, when we approach God to worship, immediately we are faced with the reality that we cannot enter His presence unless we have "clean hands and a pure heart" (Psalm 24:4). A worshiping individual is a pure individual, and a worshiping church is a pure church.

Worship demands purity. Over and over we have seen that the prerequisite to the privilege of entering God's presence is the recognition of personal sinfulness and a willingness to abandon that sinfulness. A consuming desire to be pure and clean is the normal result of being with God. The closer we draw to God, the more overwhelmed we become with our sinfulness.

The sanctity of a church or individual is the key to the quality of his worship. And conversely, the quality of our worship is the key to our own holiness. For example, the self-examination and cleansing that take place in the observance of the Communion service cannot be separated from that act of worship. The early church came to the Lord's table often—apparently even on a daily basis. Perhaps that is one reason for their spiritual power.

In fact, another hallmark of worship as God means it to be is that *the church is edified*—the saints are built up and transformed. How you worship as an individual will affect not only your life, but also the life of the church as a whole. If your worship is acceptable, the church will be strengthened and edified. But if your worship is unacceptable, the church will be weakened.

A careful examination of the book of Acts reveals that when the church was worshiping, they found favor with

God, and the Lord added to the church daily, such as should be saved. They filled the city with their doctrine. They turned the world upside down. They were winsome. They were attractive. They were dynamic.

Edification does not mean we feel better, it means we live better. The Lord purges, purifies, and builds up the church. As the saints come together to worship the Lord, they become stronger both collectively and individually, and a transformation takes place, as "we all, with unveiled face beholding as in a mirror the glory of the Lord, are being transformed into the same image from glory to glory" (2 Corinthians 3:18).

That verse is reminiscent of Moses, who had an intimate relationship with God. Exodus 33:11 says, "Thus the Lord used to speak unto Moses face to face, just as a man speaks to his friend." Moses experienced the purest, richest, most meaningful worship possible, face to face with God. God even let His glory pass before Moses—and it was a transforming experience. Afterwards, Moses' face shone. His face was so brilliantly lit that he was unrecognizable. He wasn't the man he was before. All worship has that kind of transforming effect. In holy intimacy, the true worshiper comes face to face with God, and he is transformed by the glory.

If the corporate worship in the church leaves people unchanged, the church is not really worshiping. If what goes on in the church service does not spur the saints to greater obedience, call it what you will, it isn't worship. Worship always results in a transformation, and the church is edified by it.

Finally, when we worship God acceptably, *the lost are evangelized.* The profound testimony of a worshiping individual or church has a greater impact on the lost than most sermons.

Worship, as we have seen repeatedly throughout this study, is the great purpose for the redemptive plan. The doctrine of worship, then, is the soul of evangelism. Some would separate worship from evangelism, but that is a serious error. There's nothing more important in the life of any man or woman than that his life or her life be oriented toward worshiping God for the sake of reaching others.

Jesus Himself made worship an issue in evangelism. Jesus' discourse on the importance of true worship in John 4 was not given to the Pharisees and other religious leaders. Jesus was speaking to an unbelieving, immoral woman—a prostitute. Of all the issues He could have discussed with her, the one He chose was worship. It shows the perfect way our Lord dealt personally with the needs of individuals. In the course of their brief conversation, He was able to convince her of His Messiahship, instruct her in the way of acceptable worship, and lead her to salvation.

His words on worship were exactly what the situation called for. He didn't give her a "plan" of salvation. He went right to the heart, the very essence of the matter. He first challenged her to worship God in spirit and in truth, and in doing so, He led her to faith. She believed and was redeemed, and she became a true worshiper.

When is the last time you evangelized someone in that manner? Yet an essential part of the evangelistic message is calling men and women to worship because God, the Father of the Lord Jesus Christ, is worthy of worship.

A Jewish lady went to a synagogue in the neighborhood of our church for counsel because her marriage was breaking up. They told her they couldn't counsel her until she paid her dues. Understandably, she was very upset. It happened to be a Sunday morning, and as she left the synagogue, she got caught in the crowd coming to our church and wound up inside during the service. She was so overwhelmed with the atmosphere of worship that she trusted Christ as her Savior. I baptized her a few weeks after that.

She later told me that she did not remember much about the sermon, but she was absolutely in awe of the joy and peace and love that was going on among the people as they worshiped. She had never seen anything like it. As a result of the testimony of the worshiping people she became a Christian.

It has happened again and again. As the people of God worship together, lifting their hearts to God and experiencing His infinite blessing, their faces shine because they're in His presence. That has an an impact on the people of the world that is impossible to measure. All our apologetics and evangelistic methods can never duplicate the impact of a true worshiper.

Tragically, despite all the talk about God, all the broadcasting that is done in the name of the Lord, all the people who claim to have experienced salvation, we don't see much worship as it was meant to be today. I pray we don't lose sight of it completely.

An unnamed Puritan worshiper wrote the following words that sum up the real sense of the priority of true worship:

GLORIOUS GOD,
It is the flame of my life to worship thee,
    the crown and glory of my soul to adore thee,
    heavenly pleasure to approach thee.
Give me power by thy Spirit to help me worship now,
    that I may forget the world,
    be brought into fullness of life,
    be refreshed, comforted, blessed.
Give me knowledge of thy goodness
    that I might not be over-awed by thy greatness;
Give me Jesus, Son of Man, Son of God,
    that I might not be terrified,
    but be drawn near with filial love,
    with holy boldness;
He is my mediator, brother, interpreter,
    branch, daysman, Lamb;
    him I glorify,
    in him I am set on high.
Crowns to give I have none,
    but what thou hast given I return,
    content to feel that everything is mine when it is
        thine,
    and the more fully mine when I have yielded it to
        thee.

Let me live wholly to my Saviour,
　　free from distractions,
　　from carking care,
　　from hindrances to the pursuit of the narrow way.
I am pardoned through the blood of Jesus—
　　give me a new sense of it,
　　continue to pardon me by it,
　　may I come every day to the fountain,
　　and every day be washed anew,
　　that I may worship thee always in spirit and
　　　truth.[1]

1. Arthur Bennett, *The Valley of Vision* (Carlisle, Pa.: Banner
of Truth, 1975), p. 196.